Photoshop® Elements 8
Top 100

Simplified®

TIPS & TRICKS

by Rob Sheppard

Visual

WILEY

Photoshop® Elements 8: Top 100 Simplified® Tips & Tricks

Published by
Wiley Publishing, Inc.
10475 Crosspoint Boulevard
Indianapolis, IN 46256
www.wiley.com

Published simultaneously in Canada

Trademark Acknowledgments

Contact Us

For general information on our other products and services contact our Customer Care Department within the U.S. at 877-762-2974, outside the U.S. at 317-572-3993 or fax 317-572-4002.

Wiley Publishing, Inc.

U.S. Sales

Contact Wiley at (877) 762-2974 or fax (317) 572-4002.

PRAISE FOR VISUAL BOOKS

"I have to praise you and your company on the fine products you turn out. I have twelve Visual books in my house. They were instrumental in helping me pass a difficult computer course. Thank you for creating books that are easy to follow. Keep turning out those quality books."
Gordon Justin (Brielle, NJ)

"What fantastic teaching books you have produced! Congratulations to you and your staff. You deserve the Nobel prize in Education. Thanks for helping me understand computers."
Bruno Tonon (Melbourne, Australia)

"A Picture Is Worth A Thousand Words! If your learning method is by observing or hands-on training, this is the book for you!"
Lorri Pegan-Durastante (Wickliffe, OH)

"Over time, I have bought a number of your 'Read Less - Learn More' books. For me, they are THE way to learn anything easily. I learn easiest using your method of teaching."
José A. Mazón (Cuba, NY)

"You've got a fan for life!! Thanks so much!!"
Kevin P. Quinn (Oakland, CA)

"I have several books from the Visual series and have always found them to be valuable resources."
Stephen P. Miller (Ballston Spa, NY)

"I have several of your Visual books and they are the best I have ever used."
Stanley Clark (Crawfordville, FL)

"Like a lot of other people, I understand things best when I see them visually. Your books really make learning easy and life more fun."
John T. Frey (Cadillac, MI)

"I have quite a few of your Visual books and have been very pleased with all of them. I love the way the lessons are presented!"
Mary Jane Newman (Yorba Linda, CA)

"Thank you, thank you, thank you...for making it so easy for me to break into this high-tech world."
Gay O'Donnell (Calgary, Alberta, Canada)

"I write to extend my thanks and appreciation for your books. They are clear, easy to follow, and straight to the point. Keep up the good work! I bought several of your books and they are just right! No regrets! I will always buy your books because they are the best."
Seward Kollie (Dakar, Senegal)

"I would like to take this time to thank you and your company for producing great and easy-to-learn products. I bought two of your books from a local bookstore, and it was the best investment I've ever made! Thank you for thinking of us ordinary people."
Jeff Eastman (West Des Moines, IA)

"Compliments to the chef!! Your books are extraordinary! Or, simply put, extra-ordinary, meaning way above the rest! THANKYOU THANKYOU THANKYOU! I buy them for friends, family, and colleagues."
Christine J. Manfrin (Castle Rock, CO)

CREDITS

Executive Editor
Jody Lefevere

Project Editor
Sarah Cisco

Technical Editor
Jon McFarland

Copy Editor
Lauren Kennedy

Editorial Director
Robyn Siesky

Editorial Manager
Cricket Krengel

Business Manager
Amy Knies

Senior Marketing Manager
Sandy Smith

**Vice President and Executive
Group Publisher**
Richard Swadley

**Vice President and Executive
Publisher**
Barry Pruett

Senior Project Coordinator
Lynsey Stanford

**Graphics and Production
Specialists**
Joyce Haughey
Andrea Hornberger
Jennifer Mayberry

Quality Control Technicians
John Greenough
Jessica Kramer

Proofreader
Melissa D. Buddendeck

Indexer
Sharon Shock

Screen Artist
Jill A. Proll

ABOUT THE AUTHOR

Rob Sheppard is the author/photographer of over 30 photography books, a well-known speaker and workshop leader, and editor-at-large for the prestigious *Outdoor Photographer* magazine. As author/ photographer, Sheppard has written hundreds of articles about digital photography, plus books ranging from guides to photography such as the *Magic of Digital Nature Photography* and the *National Geographic Field Guide to Digital Photography* to books about Photoshop and Lightroom including *Adobe Photoshop Lightroom 2 for Digital Photographers Only* and *Photoshop Elements 7: Top 100 Simplified Tips & Tricks.* His Web site is at www.robsheppardphoto.com and his blog is at www.photodigitary.com.

HOW TO USE THIS BOOK

Photoshop® Elements 8 Top 100 Simplified® Tips & Tricks includes 104 tasks that reveal cool secrets, teach timesaving tricks, and explain great tips guaranteed to make you more productive with Photoshop Elements. The easy-to-use layout lets you work through all the tasks from beginning to end or jump in at random.

Who is this book for?

You already know Photoshop Elements basics. Now you'd like to go beyond, with shortcuts, tricks, and tips that let you work smarter and faster. And because you learn more easily when someone *shows* you how, this is the book for you.

Conventions Used In This Book

❶ Steps

This book uses step-by-step instructions to guide you easily through each task. Numbered callouts on every screen shot show you exactly how to perform each task, step by step.

❷ Tips

Practical tips provide insights to save you time and trouble, caution you about hazards to avoid, and reveal how to do things in Photoshop Elements that you never thought possible!

❸ Task Numbers

Task numbers from 1 to 100 indicate which lesson you are working on.

❹ Difficulty Levels

For quick reference, the symbols below mark the difficulty level of each task.

DIFFICULTY LEVEL — Demonstrates a new spin on a common task

DIFFICULTY LEVEL — Introduces a new skill or a new task

DIFFICULTY LEVEL — Combines multiple skills requiring in-depth knowledge

DIFFICULTY LEVEL — Requires extensive skill and may involve other technologies

Table of Contents

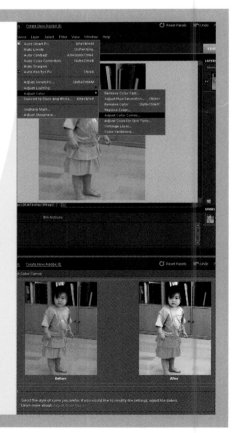

3 Work with RAW Photos in Photoshop Elements

4 Choose Local Control Features

Table of Contents

Table of Contents

⑩ Get Photos out of Photoshop Elements

Organize and Prepare Photos for Processing

Photoshop Elements 8 is the latest version of this excellent program for working with photographs on the computer. Photoshop Elements may be Photoshop's smaller sibling, but it is no second-rate program. Photoshop Elements uses the same processing engine that Photoshop uses to make your work with photos efficient and effective — but it is simpler and directly geared to photographers. And for the first time in many versions, the latest Mac and Windows versions of Photoshop Elements are the same. Everything in this book works the same with either platform except for occasional keyboard commands.

Photoshop Elements is a complete program that enables you to import images, organize them, and sort the good from the bad as well as make changes to optimize individual photos.

The order of this book follows a workflow that you can use to work efficiently in Photoshop Elements.

In this chapter, you learn what it means to develop a workflow right from the start. You can quickly import, sort, and organize your pictures so that you can find them more easily in the future. You can customize your workspace to fit your needs and interests and help you work more efficiently. You can also set preferences so that your program works its best. Do not skip over these seemingly mundane tasks because they can really help you speed up your work. Once you have practiced and learned the core controls of the program, you will find that you can work very quickly with Photoshop Elements.

Top 100

Develop a
WORKFLOW

Workflow has become a real buzzword for photographers working with their images on the computer, but it simply describes the process of how you work with images from start to finish. It is important that you develop a consistent way of working on your images that will give you reliable results.

This book is structured in such a way to show you a Photoshop Elements workflow that really does work.

Although you can skip around in the book to find specific tips, the book is ordered to follow this workflow. As you become familiar with the program, you might find that you have to adapt some of these ideas to your specific needs. Do that as long as you are getting the results you expect from your images.

- Start the process by getting your photos into Photoshop Elements in order to sort, keep, delete, and organize them. You can process individual photos without going into the Elements Organizer module of the program, but the Elements Organizer helps you manage your digital photos.

- Set the tonalities of your photos first, including blacks, whites, and midtones, and then adjust color.

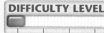

● Fix problems in your photos such as wrong colors, defects in an image, sensor dust, and so on.

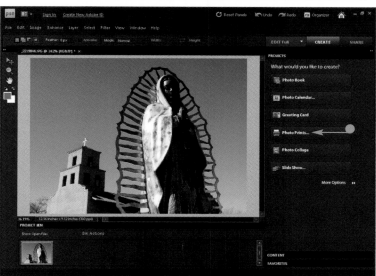

● Consider how you want to share your photos with others, including prints, photo books, Web galleries, e-mail, and much more.

TIPS

Did You Know?

Photoshop Elements was originally designed to make Photoshop more accessible for photographers. Photoshop was first developed to help people work on photos on the computer, not for photographers. Photoshop Elements has always had the photographer as the primary focus of its development and enhancement.

Try This!

Make your image immediately fill the central work area by pressing Ctrl/Cmd+0 (if you press Ctrl/Cmd+O, you get an Open dialog box). You can do this when a photo first comes into the program edit space or when you have enlarged a portion of the photo and need to go back to seeing all of it.

Did You Know?

Editing photos used to mean picking the good from the bad. When Photoshop was developed, the computer folks decided to call the changes to the images *editing*, so there is confusion about what editing really is for the photographer. This book avoids both usages and specifically describes the process being used.

IMPORT
your images

In order to work on your images, you must get them onto your computer and recognized by Photoshop Elements. To use the Organizer in Photoshop Elements, you have to tell the program how to deal with your photos. It needs, in a sense, a map to where your photos are located. Photoshop Elements can help you import your photos from memory card to hard drive, including copying them from the card into a specific folder and renaming the files, as well as having Organizer recognize them. Or you can tell

Photoshop Elements to recognize photographs that are already on your computer.

When you first open Photoshop Elements, click the Organizer button to go into the Organizer mode. All importing is done through this mode. Once the Organizer recognizes the images, they appear as thumbnails on your screen, which you can then sort, place into albums, and generally place them in an order that makes them easy to locate.

Importing from a Digital Camera or Memory Card

① Click File.

② Click Get Photos and Videos.

③ Click From Camera or Card Reader.

The Photo Downloader dialog box appears.

④ Click here to select your camera or card reader.

⑤ Click Browse to select where you want the photos to go on your hard drive.

Navigate to the folder you want to use in the directory tree that appears.

6 Click Make New Folder for a new group of photos.

7 Name your new folder.

8 Click OK.

2

DIFFICULTY LEVEL

9 Click here to select or create subfolders in the new folder, such as ones based on dates photos were shot, or choose None.

10 Click here to rename your photos or keep the original file names.

11 Type a new name for your photos if needed.

12 Click here to leave photos on the memory card so that your camera can reformat the card properly.

13 Click Get Photos.

The photos will now be imported into your computer and included in the Organizer.

14 When the Files Successfully Copied dialog box opens, click yes.

TIPS

Did You Know?

A quality memory card reader is the fastest and most dependable way to download images. A card reader needs no power, can be left connected to your computer, and will not be damaged if accidentally knocked to the floor.

Did You Know?

The Automatic Download check box in the Photo Downloader dialog box sets up your computer to automatically download photos based on criteria set in Preferences, found in the Edit menu for PCs and the Photoshop Elements menu for Macs. This can be a problem because it does not enable you to put photos into specific folders for each download, nor does it enable you to rename photos.

Did You Know?

Most photographers prefer to put images into distinct file folders on their hard drives instead of lumping them together into the Pictures folder. Photo Downloader enables you set up specific folders based on date and location. For example, you can put photos in a folder called Digital Photos on your hard drive to make them easier to find if the Organizer in Photoshop Elements ever fails.

IMPORT
your images

Sometimes you will have groups of photos on your memory card that you do not want to mix together into a single folder. It can be very helpful to keep your photos separated by folders so that you can always find images on your hard drive, even without Photoshop Elements. The program gives you the option to import only the pictures that you want from a memory card in an advanced dialog box. This dialog box is very similar to the Photo Downloader dialog box, but it includes some additional choices you should know about.

Photoshop Elements also enables you to import images already on your hard drive. The process is very similar, but does use a different dialog box. This can be useful when you have transferred pictures directly from one computer to another, for example.

Advanced Importing from a Digital Camera or Memory Card

① Repeat steps 1 to 4 from the "Importing from a Digital Camera or Memory Card" section to open the Photo Downloader dialog box.

② Click Advanced Dialog.

The advanced Photo Downloader dialog box appears.

③ Click Check All to import all photos.

④ Click UnCheck All to deselect all photos to select specific images for import.

⑤ Click the first photo of your group to import.

6 Scroll down to the last photo in the group.

7 Shift+click that last photo to select all photos from the first one to this one, but no others.

Press Ctrl/Cmd+click isolated photos to add or remove them from the group.

8 Click the check box under any image to check all that are selected.

9 Click here to open Advanced Options if it is not already open.

● A good option to select is Import into Album (☐ changes to ☑) if you have albums set up.

10 Click here to open Apply Metadata if it is not already open.

11 Click here to select Basic Metadata.

12 Type your name for the Creator and Copyright text boxes.

13 Click Get Photos.

The photos will now be imported to your computer and included in the Organizer.

TIPS

Did You Know?

When the Organizer recognizes photos, Photoshop Elements does not move or change them unless you tell it to. Photoshop Elements is simply creating a map to these image files on your hard drive so that it can find and organize the photos as needed.

Try This!

Use the Light Bulb icons (💡). Photoshop Elements scatters tips throughout the program to help you when you do not understand a particular control or option. Click the icon and a tip appears, providing information on how to use the control or option.

Did You Know?

Having your name and copyright information on a photo helps people keep track of your photos. Even if you are not a pro, having your name in the metadata means that if you give your photo files to someone, such as for an organization's brochure, everyone will know whose photos they are.

VIEW PHOTOS
with full-screen mode

The Organizer in Photoshop Elements is great for seeing a whole lot of photos at once. This can help you check out your latest photo shoot as well as visually find important images. But seeing larger images enables you to find the best photos, whether it means checking sharpness, focus, a person's expression, and so on.

While you have always been able to look at larger versions of your photo in previous versions of the

software, Photoshop Elements 8 now includes a full-featured full-screen mode. This mode removes all distractions from your monitor so you can focus just on your image. This truly makes the image the star and puts the software in the background. This can make it easier to evaluate your photos after importing them because you can easily move from one photo to the next.

① Click a photo that you wish to see Full Screen.

② Click the Full-Screen icon, the little monitor with a playback arrow.

A full-screen image appears.

● The playback toolbar also appears at the bottom of the screen.

③ Click the arrows to move the display of photos forward or backward from the whole group in Organizer.

A new photo appears.

4 Move your cursor to the left side to open the Quick Organize panel.

Use the Quick Organize panel for quickly adding keywords or putting a photo into an album.

5 Click the filmstrip icon on the bottom toolbar.

A filmstrip appears.

● The active photo is highlighted in blue in the filmstrip and also appears enlarged in the main work area.

6 Click any image in the filmstrip to display it large.

7 Press the Escape key to go back to Organizer.

TIPS

Did You Know?

The full-screen view can be used as a slide show. Click the center arrow of the bottom toolbar to start playing images or pause the slide show. You can change how long each image is on the screen as well as play music with the photos by clicking the Wrench icon, which gives you settings to try. You can only play this slide show when the Photoshop Elements program is open.

Try This!

The full-screen playback can be very helpful, but sometimes you want to go back and forth between the Organizer multi-image view and the full-screen view. You can do this quickly and easily with the function key F11. Press F11 to go from Organizer to Full Screen, and then press the Escape key to go back to Organizer.

Did You Know?

The Quick Edit panel in the full-screen view can be a useful way to quickly make adjustments to your photos. Move your cursor over the Quick Edit bar to expand the panel. Then choose controls that will enable you to adjust your photo.

SORT
the good pictures from the bad

Traditionally, going through your pictures, finding the good ones and getting rid of the bad has been called photo editing. However, when computer engineers developed programs like Photoshop, they decided to call changing pictures in those programs photo editing too, so the term can be confusing. Still, you do need to go through your pictures and edit them based on the original definition of the word.

Photoshop Elements gives you some excellent tools to do just that. You can compare pictures, look at pictures in different sizes, and discover which pictures work well for you and which do not. To save hard drive space and eliminate clutter there, you should delete images that really do not satisfy you, thus reducing the number of pictures you have to go through to find the really good ones.

Set Up Your View of the Photos

1 Click and drag the thumbnail slider to change the sizes of your photo thumbnails.

2 Press Ctrl/Cmd+click photos to select images that you want to rotate.

3 Click the appropriate Rotate icon to rotate the selected photos.

4 Select the Details check box to show ratings (☐ changes to ✓).

Note: You can also click the View menu and then View Details to show ratings.

5 Click the stars to rate your photos.

You can use a system such as one star for those photos you reject, five stars for the best ones, and various numbers of stars in between to define which photos you like or dislike.

Delete Photos You Do Not Want

6 Click one rating star in the upper right of the thumbnail display.

7 To limit photos to only those with one star, click the box to the right of the stars and select only.

8 Select all photos with Ctrl+A.

9 Press Delete.

The Confirm Deletion from Catalog dialog box appears.

10 Select the Also delete selected item(s) from the hard disk check box to throw out your rejects (☐ changes to ☑).

Make sure the Also delete selected item(s) from the hard disk check box is deselected to only remove photos from Photoshop Elements view (☑ changes to ☐).

● If you feel that you made a mistake, you can click Cancel and change the ratings.

11 Click OK to finish the process.

12 Click Show All to get your photos on screen again.

DIFFICULTY LEVEL

TIPS

Remember!

You can delete images from Photoshop Elements and/or off your computer altogether. Simply select the image you want to remove and press Delete. This opens a dialog box that enables you to decide if you simply want to remove the photo from Photoshop Elements' view or remove it from the hard drive completely.

Try This!

To see any image at a large size, double-click it. This shows you the photo filling the thumbnail area without any other photos. This helps you better see details in your photos, such as sharpness or exposure problems. Double-click the image again to go back to the thumbnail view.

Did You Know?

You can show file names and other detail using the View menu. Click View and then select the appropriate menu item to show these details in your thumbnail display.

STACK
your images

Most people who enjoy digital photography take advantage of the fact that once you own the camera and memory card, there is no cost for taking pictures. This means you can freely photograph a subject, trying different angles or varied techniques. However, as you do this, you accumulate a lot of similar photos in your digital files. That can make working with a particular group of photos more challenging because you have to look at a lot of similar images before you come to the new ones.

Stacking is a new Photoshop Elements 8 feature. It enables you to place special subgroups of your photos into stacks that then display as if they were one image. This can simplify the view of your photos in Organizer. You can also use stacks to keep a particular small group of photos together.

① Click the first image of a group that could be stacked.

② Shift+click the last image of that group.

The whole group is now selected.

③ Click Edit.

The Edit menu opens.

④ Select Stack.

⑤ Select Stack Selected Photos.

The images are visually stacked so you see only one.

● The Stack icon appears in the upper-right corner of the stack to inform you it is a stack.

6 Click the small arrow at the middle of the right side of the photo thumbnail.

The stack opens and is highlighted as a group.

7 Click the small arrow at the middle of the right side of the last photo to collapse the stack again.

TIPS

Compare!

Many times you will find that two photos look similar and you simply want to find and keep the best. You do not necessarily want or need a stack. Photoshop Elements has a great tool that enables you to compare photos two at a time. Select two photos, and then click the Display button at the top right of the interface and select Compare Photos Side by Side. The two photos will now be displayed full screen next to each other.

Try This!

You can also use stacking to simplify and organize your thumbnail view. For example, you could stack photos of each child at a birthday party so that the entire group of party photos is organized into stacks based on individuals. Pressing Ctrl/Cmd+ click isolates photos to select them.

Did You Know?

Stacking is simply another way to group photos so they are useful to you. It is based on an old technique slide shooters used when sorting photos. They would pile similar slides on top of each other, making stacks that kept their light tables better organized.

CREATE ALBUMS
to group your pictures

Albums are groupings of pictures based on your needs. You can create albums based on events such as birthdays, locations such as a recently visited city, family members, and much more.

Albums enable you to quickly find pictures even if they are part of a very large collection of images. They also enable you to group pictures together even if they were not taken at the same time. For example, you could set up an album based on a child's name

and then put images of that child into that album. If you did this over time, you would have a collection of images of that child from many different times and places.

Albums do not duplicate photographs. They only create references to where the pictures are on your hard drive. For that reason, individual pictures could be in many albums, which can help you find them faster in different ways.

❶ Ctrl+click photos to select individual images, or click a photo and then Shift+click the last image in a group to select photos in order.

You can also press Ctrl/Cmd+A to select all photos.

❷ Click the large green plus sign under Albums and select New Album to add an album.

● You can open the Albums section of the task panel by clicking the arrow next to the word Albums.

The Album Details panel appears.

❸ You can group albums by using the Album Group function, but start with None (Top Level).

❹ Type a name for your album.

❺ Deselect the Backup/Synchronize check box until you have a Photoshop.com account (☑ changes to ☐).

● Your selected photos appear in the Content box.

DIFFICULTY LEVEL

6 Click an image and drag it into the Content box to add it to an album.

Note: Neither adding nor deleting photos from an album affects their position on the hard drive.

7 Click Done.

The new album now appears in the Albums panel.

8 Click the album to select it.

● The photos you put in the album now appear with a small icon below them to indicate they are in albums.

9 To see that icon, select Details (☐ changes to ☑).

● You can edit your album by clicking the Edit icon.

 TIPS

Did You Know?

You can add photos to an album at any time. Whenever you see a photo that belongs in an album, click it and then drag it to the album. It is automatically placed in the album and will appear there whenever that album is opened. Remember you are only creating references to photos and not actually moving any.

Try This!

You can immediately put any new photos just imported into Photoshop Elements into an album. Select all images in that new group of photos, add an album with a name appropriate to that group, and the photos should appear in the Contents box. If not, select and drag the new pictures into that Item box.

Smart Albums!

You can create a smart album that automatically adds photos to the album. You set up criteria, such as file names, keywords, and camera type, in the New Smart Album dialog box, which you access by clicking the Albums plus sign (➕). Whenever a photo with those criteria appears in Photoshop Elements, it is automatically included in the smart album.

USE KEYWORDS
to tag your images

Keywords are words that you add to your photo's metadata (information about the image held in the file). They can be a useful way for you to organize and find your pictures because keywords are searchable. Albums are great for creating large groupings of pictures that you can readily access. With keywords and the search function in Organizer, you can go to specific images depending on the keywords you have used.

Keywords can be as detailed as you want. You can simply add words to large groups of pictures, which makes this process easier. Or if you want to be able to really find specific images, you can add a lot of very specific keywords to individual pictures.

Regardless of how you use keywords, they are still an important part of Photoshop Elements to understand and use as needed.

① Click the arrow in front of Keyword Tags to open the keyword part of the Organize task panel.

● For more space, close Albums by clicking the arrow by that title.

② You can start with the keywords that are listed.

③ Click the large green plus sign under Keyword Tags.

A drop-down menu appears.

● You can choose New Sub-Category or New Category to create your own category for keywords.

④ Select New Keyword Tag to add a keyword.

The Create Keyword
Tag dialog box appears.

⑤ Choose a category.

⑥ Type a name for your
keyword tag.

⑦ Choose an icon if
desired by clicking the
Edit Icon.

The Edit Keyword Tag Icon dialog
box appears.

⑧ Click Import to look for
something to use as an icon.

● The Import Image for Keyword
Tag Icon dialog box appears.

⑨ Find a photo that looks
interesting, perhaps from the
same group of images.

⑩ Click Open to select this photo
for your icon.

⑪ Click OK to use this new icon for
your keywords.

*Note: It is not required to have an
icon for every keyword tag.*

⑫ Click OK again to accept the
changes to the Create Keyword
Tag dialog box.

TIPS

Try This!
When all the task panel controls
are open, your interface can get
cluttered and confusing. Click the
little arrows at the left of the panel
category titles to open and close a
category of control, such as
Albums. Simplify the workspace by
closing panel categories you are
not using.

Important!
Pick keywords that help you find
your photos. Your keywords will be
unique to your type of
photography. Adding keywords
that others use but do not fit your
images will make your searches
confusing. Ask yourself, "What do I
need to find?" in order to create
keywords that work for you and
your needs.

Customize It!
You can add as much or as little
information as you want to
keyword tags. The Create Keyword
Tag dialog box includes the option
to add notes or a specific address
for a location. These are not
requirements, only options that
some photographers will use
frequently, and others not at all.
Use what you need and what
works for you.

USE KEYWORDS
to tag your images

Keywords are one of those things that many photographers put off creating. The best time to add keywords is when you first import pictures into Photoshop Elements. At that time, you remember the most about your pictures. It is also easier to add keywords at this time because all your pictures are right in front of you.

It is important to understand that you can add keyword tags to one picture and only one picture, to a few, or to hundreds. Keywords enable you to be very specific, down to putting a specific name on something that appears only in one picture. They also enable you to be broader in your approach and put a single word across a whole group of pictures so that you can find that group again. Keywords work across all pictures within Organizer so that you can find pictures throughout Organizer by simply searching for keywords.

- A new keyword tag appears in the category you chose in step 5.

⑬ Select the photos that need this keyword.

The selected photos have a blue frame around them.

⑭ Click and drag the selected photos onto the tag and they gain that tag.

You can click and drag multiple times, with different groups of photos, to add more keyword tags to photos.

- A small keyword tag icon appears below your photos.

⑮ To put a keyword on specific photos, click the tag.

⑯ Drag the tag and drop it on the photo.

When more than one keyword tag is added to a photo, the icon at the lower right of the image changes to a Yellow Tag icon.

⑰ Find specific images based on your keyword by selecting the box in front of a specific keyword tag.

⑱ Click additional tags to narrow your search.

⑲ To show specific items in an album, click the album before selecting Keyword Tags.

⑳ To search for images throughout your image files, click Show All first.

㉑ Type a name in the search box to show photos related to that name quickly.

TIPS

Customize It!

Take any existing keyword tag and customize it for your needs. Right-click any keyword tag to get a context-sensitive menu. This enables you to edit your keyword or keyword category, add a new keyword to the category, add a new sub-category, or remove keywords or categories as needed.

Did You Know?

Photoshop Elements includes a special feature that enables you to find people in your photos for tagging. This is found in the Keyword Tags category of the task panel. You will see an icon with a person in a little photo (▣). Hover your cursor over it and you will see "Start people recognition." Click it and all photos with faces are highlighted for you.

Try This!

You can type a list of keywords based on common descriptions of things in your photos. You can then import this list into Photoshop Elements by clicking the large green plus sign (➕) under Keyword Tags and selecting From File. This file must be an XML (Extensible Markup Language) file. You can save a Word file as an XML file for this purpose.

FIND PHOTOS
with face recognition

Keywords are a great tool to help you find specific subjects or types of photos. They do require you to set the keyword and find the appropriate photos for them. Many photographers like to identify people in their photos so they can find them later based on specific individuals in the images.

With Photoshop Elements 8, you now can tell the program to "recognize" people in your photos for you. Face recognition can help you quickly go through

photos to find specific instances of a person and add keywords for them. The program does a pretty good job of finding faces in everything, including portraits, group photos, and small people in larger scenes. You can even have Photoshop Elements highlight all the faces it can see as faces so you can give keywords for the individuals.

① Click an album to analyze for faces.

② Select all images by pressing Ctrl/Cmd+A.

③ Click the Edit menu.

④ Select Run Auto Analyzer.

Photoshop Elements analyzes your group of photos for faces and other similarities.

⑤ Click OK in the Analysis completed dialog box that appears.

⑥ Click the Face Recognition icon in the Keyword Tags panel.

The People Recognition window opens.

- A new person has a white square around her face with the message, "Who is this?"

⑦ Click "Who is this?" and type the person's name.

⑧ Click the arrows at the left and right to move backward or forward in the group of photos.

- If Photoshop Elements recognizes the person, it asks you to confirm if this is that person.

⑨ Click the green check mark if the name is correct.

If Photoshop Elements does not recognize the person, it will ask again "Who is this?"

Click the message and fill in the person's name.

⑩ Click Done when you have assigned all the names.

TIPS

Did You Know?

Software companies have been trying to develop advanced face recognition for many years. There is a big demand for it in security markets. The ability to quickly scan security videos, for example, to watch for terrorists or other threatening travelers would be a huge benefit for security agencies.

Try This!

Right-clicking a mouse is standard procedure for PC users. It is an efficient and quick way to access important contextual menus. However, for a long time, Apple did not use a right-click mouse, even though programs supported it. Today, all Mac users, whether they program an Apple mouse for right-click functionality or buy another brand, need to have and use a right-click mouse.

Did You Know?

All the organizing tools shown in this chapter are simply that—tools. You have to supply the organization; Photoshop Elements does not. Organize your photos using Albums and Keyword Tags to mimic how you file anything. Following a plan that is true to your own organizational methods is more likely to create a system that will be versatile and efficient for you.

CHANGE THE ORGANIZER
interface as needed

Photoshop Elements has been designed for photographers and its interface reflects that. However, every photographer has unique needs and ways of working. You can change the way the interface for Organizer looks, and consequently acts, to customize it for your needs.

The controls that affect the look of the interface are buttons in the top menu bars, such as Thumbnail Size icons, and in the View and Window menus. Do not be afraid to try different looks for your interface — you can always change back to the original look by clicking the button or menu item a second time.

However you set up your interface, it should be something that helps you work more efficiently. Do not simply use something because it is available or someone else uses it. Be sure that it really helps your work in the program. Working in Photoshop Elements should be a fun way of interacting with your pictures.

① Click the Display button to change your display views.

② Click Folder Location view to show a directory tree.

③ In the Folder Location view, you can click directly on a folder to find photos.

If Photoshop Elements is not managing pictures in a folder, right-click the folder to add them.

④ Change your thumbnail size with the thumbnail slider.

#9

⑤ Click here to expand or collapse the panel section.

⑥ Click and drag along an interface edge to make it larger or smaller.

⑦ Click Window to change what appears in the interface.

⑧ Click Hide Task Pane for a large image viewing area; click Show Task Pane for the normal view.

 TIPS

Did You Know?

You can control many features of Photoshop Elements with keyboard commands. These enable you to quickly access controls with just a couple of keystrokes. These keystrokes are listed next to the controls in the menus. For example, you can turn on and off the detail display for thumbnails by pressing Ctrl+D.

Try This!

The Timeline in Photoshop Elements can help you find photos by date. You can turn it on in the Window menu. It works for the entire database, so click the Show All button at the top left of the thumbnails first. Then select a specific time and photos appear below from that time. You can also drag the left and right sliders to limit the dates to show images.

Did You Know?

By default, all thumbnails have a small white border around them to make them show up better. Not everyone likes this border, but it can easily be turned off. Go to the View menu and click Show Borders around Thumbnails.

SET PREFERENCES
to make Organizer work for you

You can use Photoshop Elements right out of the box and get good results. However, the program has some preferences worth considering that enable you to fine-tune how it works with your computer and your needs.

Photoshop Elements has two sets of preferences, one for the Organizer and one for the Editor. In both cases, they appear at the bottom of the Edit menu. You can leave many of the choices at their default settings, but you might want to tweak some to refine how Photoshop Elements works for you. Many of the settings are self-explanatory. If you are not sure of something and want to try it, go ahead, because all the settings can be reset with the Restore Default Settings button at the bottom of the dialog box. Just reopen Preferences and use this button to go back to the defaults. This section offers some specific options that are especially worth looking at.

1 Click Edit to open the Edit menu.

2 Select Preferences.

3 Select General.

The Preferences dialog box appears.

4 Adjust the User Interface Brightness and Grid Brightness to make the background lighter or darker.

5 Choose the order to show images by date (○ changes to ●).

6 Select a preferred Date Format (○ changes to ●).

● You can click any category to adjust specific preferences.

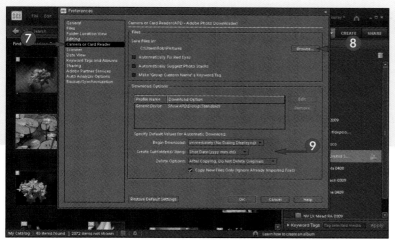

⑦ Click Camera or Card Reader.

⑧ Click the Browse button to select a default location for your image files as they are copied from your camera or card reader.

⑨ Specify default settings for automatic downloading. The settings shown are a good starting point.

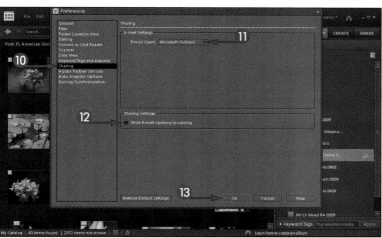

⑩ Click Sharing to set up e-mail with Photoshop Elements.

⑪ Choose your E-mail Client program.

⑫ Select Write E-mail captions to catalog to record and save captions (☐ changes to ✔).

⑬ Click OK to close the Preferences dialog box.

TIPS

Did You Know?

You can have images in a separate location not connected to your computer and still reference them in Organizer. Photoshop Elements keeps a small thumbnail for each of the images so that you can still see them in thumbnail view. You can change the size of these previews in the Files section of Preferences.

Try This!

Select photos by standard computer-selection commands. Pressing Ctrl/Cmd+A selects all photos currently displayed in the organizer. Pressing Ctrl/Cmd+clicking photos selects them one after another. Click one photo, and then Shift+click farther down; all photos in between are selected. You can also deselect a selected photo by Ctrl+clicking it.

Customize It!

If you use a lot of keywords, you can customize the way they are sorted in Preferences, in the Keyword Tags and Albums section. You can, for example, change how the keywords are sorted, either alphabetically or manually. You can also choose how the tag icons are used, and display or hide hints for face recognition.

BACK UP YOUR PICTURES
to protect them

Whenever you read about fires and other disasters destroying people's property, you always read about people wanting to save their photo albums. Photos are important to us in so many ways, whether they are memories of children growing up or artistic visions of a great natural setting.

Digital photos are vulnerable to loss from a hard drive failure — and hard drives do fail. Plus, without a hard copy, you have no other record of the images. By backing them up, you can add more security to your

pictures than is possible with traditional film. It is very easy to back up your photos onto accessory hard drives that plug in to your computer. These have come down so much in price that many photographers back up their pictures on more than one.

Backup is so important that Adobe has added special backup features to Photoshop Elements 8, which will be covered in Task #94. You should have some backup system of your own that you can control and access easily, which is covered here.

An external hard drive is one of the best ways to back up the images on your computer's hard drive.

Back Up to an External Hard Drive

1. Click the Display button in the top menu bar.

2. Select Folder Location.

3. Find a folder you want to duplicate for backup in the folder tree.

4 If necessary, reveal the external hard drive using the right slider.

5 Click the folder you want to duplicate.

6 Drag the folder to the external hard drive.

The folder is saved on the external hard drive.

Use Backup Software

Note: *You can obtain special backup software to help you with backing up your photos.*

1 With your backup software open, choose the folder or folders you want to back up.

2 Click the Folder icon to find your folder.

3 Choose the accessory drive for backup.

4 Click the Folder icon to select the location for backup.

5 Click Run Now to start the backup.

TIPS

Did You Know?
Backup software can make your backups easier. Once you set up backup software for specific folders and a specific accessory drive, the software remembers those locations. The next time that you ask it to back up, it simply compares what is in those two locations and adds only what is new.

Try This!
Small portable hard drives designed for laptops are more expensive than other accessory hard drives. However, they can be handy for accessing your photographs from your laptop or other computer. In addition, you can easily store such a hard drive in a location separate from your main computer, giving you added protection.

Try This!
You can create a duplicate file structure on your backup drive as you can on your main computer. Simply create folders and levels of folders that are the same on both. For example, if your photos are structured by year and then by specific event, then use the same year and event structure. Then you can simply copy a folder from one drive to another in the same filing setup.

Start Adjusting Your Images in Photoshop Elements

A digital camera is an interesting bit of technology. It does a great job of capturing an image from the world, but this image is not necessarily a correct interpretation of that world. The camera is limited by the capabilities of its sensor, how the camera engineers have designed its internal processing, and its lens. The engineers must create image-capture capabilities that meet the needs of a wide range of users, so the camera is rarely perfect for any one photographer.

That is where Photoshop Elements comes in. With most images, you will need to spend some time tweaking them so they accurately reflect what you originally saw. In this chapter you learn some basic steps to get your photos looking more the way you expect a photograph to look. This chapter also reflects a workflow from start to finish that you can use as you work on your pictures. A few of the steps, such as setting blacks and whites, adjusting midtones, and color correction, are important steps for any photograph.

Top 100

Open pictures and
USE SAVE AS

To start the process of working on photos in Photoshop Elements, you need to get a picture into the Editor workspace of Photoshop Elements. You can work with Organizer or you can get images directly into Editor from the Editor's File menu. The advantage of working with Organizer is that you have access to lots of pictures at once. If you are working with a specific picture and you know exactly where it is on your hard drive, opening the picture directly in Editor can be easier.

Many photographers worry about adversely affecting an image and, therefore, are cautious when working on it. If you immediately save any picture as a new file when it is opened into Photoshop Elements, you are protecting your original image file. This frees you to work on your image without worrying about permanently damaging it. You cannot damage your original because you are not working on it at this point.

1 Click a photo to select it.

2 Click the down arrow in the Fix tab.

3 Select Full Photo Edit.

The photo appears in Editor.

4 Click File.

5 Select Save As.

The Save As dialog box appears.

6 Choose a location to save your photos.

7 Give your photo a name that makes sense to you.

8 Choose either Photoshop (.psd) or TIFF (.tif) for the format.

9 Uncheck Save in Version Set with Original unless you have good reasons to keep all of your versions with the original file.

10 Click Save.

If you chose Photoshop in step 8, your photo is saved without any additional steps.

If you chose TIFF in step 8, you will see Save Options choices.

11 Click Save and the TIFF Options dialog box appears.

12 Select None (O changes to ●) for image compression, although LZW can be used if your photos will be opened only in Elements.

● Leave the radio buttons in the Pixel Order and Byte Order sections at the default settings.

13 Click OK.

TIPS

Try This!

You can open photos directly from Editor. Click File and then choose Open. This takes you to the Open dialog box. Navigate to where your digital photos are kept, and then find the folder and the image. When you click a photo once to select it, a preview appears. Click Open to open it in Editor.

Did You Know?

Photographers should save images in Photoshop, TIFF, and JPEG formats. You should not use JPEG as a working file format; that is, one that you use to work on images while you are in Editor. JPEG is a compressed file format and should be used only for archiving images when you need to keep file sizes small or for e-mail and Web purposes. The Photoshop format is ideal because it enables you to do all kinds of work on a picture and save everything, including layers, when you save the file. The TIFF format is good for when you need to open pictures in other programs, such as Word or Publisher. Both Photoshop and TIFF enable you to open, adjust, and save an image as much as you want without any loss of quality.

MAKE THE EDITOR INTERFACE
your own

The Editor interface of Photoshop Elements is very adaptable. Most photographers find it helpful to make some adjustments to that interface so that the program works better for them. One adjustment you might do right away is how Effects and Undo History are displayed. Adobe put Effects in the right-side palette bin as a default rather than Undo History. Although many photographers use Effects, almost all use Undo History.

In this task, you learn to create an efficient workspace suitable for most photographers. You also learn how to add or subtract panels from the interface so you can do your own customization.

You can always turn on or off parts of the interface by selecting items in the Window menu. Do not be afraid to deselect parts of the interface that you do not use or select something that seems useful for your purposes even if it is not included here. You can also reset the interface in the Window menu by clicking Reset Panels.

① Click the Effects bar to the right of the Effects tab.

② Drag the Effects panel from the panel bin.

③ Click the X at the upper right to close the panel.

● The Undo History panel appears in the panel bin.

TIPS

Try This!

The Project Bin at the bottom of the interface shows the active images in Photoshop Elements, whether there is one or more. If you want more working space, you can always hide this panel. Simply double-click anywhere along the bar that includes the Project Bin tab. To bring the bin back, double-click again.

Try This!

You can make the Undo History panel larger or smaller in the palette bin. Click and drag the separating line between it and the Layers palette; the cursor changes to a small double arrow when you are over the right spot. You can also make your palette bin larger or smaller by clicking and dragging the left edge.

Did You Know?

Adobe deliberately chose the dark gray interface of Photoshop Elements. This color sets pictures off well and makes them the stars of the interface. In addition, the neutral color does not compete with or affect people's perception of colors in a photograph.

SET PREFERENCES
to make Editor work for you

Just as in the Organizer (see task #10), Editor has preferences you can set to make the program run more efficiently with the computer. They are in the same place in the menu as they are in Organizer: under the Edit menu, at the bottom of the menu. You can use all the defaults in the preferences and still have good results. Adobe put a lot of thought into the defaults, so they do work. However, a lot of them are based on what most people might choose, but not necessarily what you would choose.

In Preferences, you can choose to affect all sorts of things, including how files are saved, the performance of Photoshop Elements with your computer, plug-ins, and more. Most of the options are fairly self-explanatory, and if you are not sure what they do, you can always try them and then reset everything later if needed.

① Click Edit, select Preferences, and then click General to open the Preferences dialog box.

You can leave most of the General settings at the default selections.

② Deselect the Export Clipboard check box (☑ changes to ☐) to keep the Clipboard empty except when you want something copied to it.

③ Select Save Panel Locations to save your interface configuration (☐ changes to ☑).

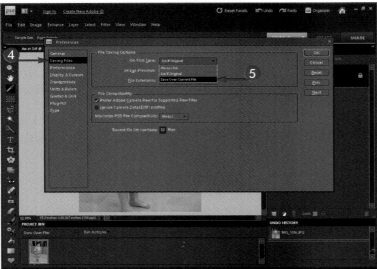

④ Click Saving Files.

⑤ From the On First Save drop-down menu, select Save Over Current File for efficient work or Always Ask if you want to be extra safe.

The defaults work well for the remaining options.

6 Click Performance.

7 Under Memory Usage, set the usage in the Let Photoshop Elements Use field to the highest number shown in the Ideal Range unless you have less than 1GB of RAM.

This setting is not completed until Photoshop Elements is closed and opened again.

8 Select any accessory drives under Scratch Disks to ensure you have scratch space (☐ changes to ☑).

DIFFICULTY LEVEL

9 Click Display & Cursors.

10 Select how your brush will display with painting cursors (○ changes to ●).

You can keep the defaults to start, but change this later if you prefer, for example, a precise cursor.

11 Select Show Crosshair in Brush Tip to show the center of a working brush (☐ changes to ☑).

12 Click OK to close the Preferences dialog box.

TIPS

Did You Know?

When Photoshop Elements runs out of RAM or "thinking space," it needs someplace to work, and uses space on a hard drive. This is called *scratch space*, and the drive being used is the *scratch drive*. It can be helpful to have more than one drive designated for scratch space so that Photoshop Elements never runs out of room to think.

More Options!

Color Settings are a group of preferences that have their own separate settings. They are accessed in the Edit menu, too. You will do okay when they are set at the defaults, but you get more capabilities and options for how color can be adjusted if you select Always Optimize for Printing. This gives you what is called the AdobeRGB color space.

Did You Know?

A color space is something a computer uses to describe how colors are rendered. A common color space for JPEG files is sRGB, which works fine for many images but is a smaller color space than Adobe RGB. Adobe RGB gives you more flexibility and options when you are adjusting color and tonality.

EXPERIMENT TO LEARN
more about controls

Many photographers get very cautious when working on pictures in Photoshop Elements. That is actually not the best way to work. An experimental approach shows you what controls do or do not do to a picture very quickly, whereas a more cautious approach may limit you because you do not see the possibilities.

Sometimes it is hard to remember all the controls Photoshop Elements. You do not have to remember

all of them perfectly. In fact, a great way of learning the program is simply to try them out. Experiment. See what happens. Then simply press Ctrl/Cmd+Z to undo anything that you have done.

As you see in task #13, you cannot really hurt your pictures. Experimenting frees you to look for possibilities so that you can get the most out of your pictures.

Experiment with Levels

① Click Enhance.

② Select Adjust Lighting.

③ Select Levels.

The Levels dialog box opens.

④ Click the black slider and move it to the right.

⑤ Click the gray slider and move it to the right.

This makes the photo darker.

● Click Reset to reset the sliders at any time.

⑥ Click Cancel.

1. Click Enhance.

2. Select Adjust Color.

3. Select Adjust Color Curves.

DIFFICULTY LEVEL

The Adjust Color Curves dialog box appears.

4. Click and drag the Adjust Highlights slider far to the right.

5. Click and drag the Adjust Shadows slider far to the left.

The image gets very contrasty.

● Click Reset at any time.

6. Click Cancel.

TIPS

Did You Know?

Dialog boxes are not always in the best places on the screen when they open. Frequently, they cover up important parts of the picture. You can easily move the dialog box to a different location by clicking the top bar of the dialog box and then dragging it to a new location.

Test It!

You can quickly see the before-and-after versions of your picture when you are making adjustments. Also, all dialog boxes for adjustments include a small check box for the option called Preview. Select and deselect this box to see what the picture looks like with and without the adjustments. When Preview is selected, you see what the adjustments look like.

Get Help!

Dialog boxes in Photoshop Elements frequently include a Learn About link that refers specifically to the control you are working with. This is a great resource. Simply click the blue word that describes the function of your dialog box to open a help page explaining it.

YOU CANNOT HURT
your pictures

Another reason many photographers are cautious when working on pictures in Photoshop Elements is that they are afraid of hurting their images. You cannot really hurt your pictures. This is an important thing to keep in mind because it frees you to work more confidently with your pictures.

As long as you have done a Save As for your original image (see task #12), you cannot hurt the original image because you are now working on copy. And as you work, you can always undo everything that you have already done. As long as you do not save what you have done, there is no change made to the file you are working on except within Photoshop Elements. The Undo History palette gives you even more options for undoing your adjustments. Knowing this can help you experiment without restraint and discover the possibilities for your image.

Reverse Adjustments

① Click Edit.

② Select Undo Levels.

Note: Alternately, press Ctrl/Cmd+Z.

③ Select Revert to go back to the last saved version of the open file.

Reset a Dialog Box

① Click Enhance, select Adjust Color, and then select Adjust Hue/Saturation.

② Randomly make some adjustments with Hue/Saturation. You do not have to know what you are doing.

③ Press and hold the Alt key and what was the Cancel button changes into a Reset button.

④ Click Reset to bring the adjustments back to their default settings.

⑤ Close the dialog box.

Use Undo History

1 Click Enhance.

2 Randomly make some adjustments from Adjust Lighting and Adjust Color. You do not have to know what you are doing.

● All adjustments appear in the Undo History palette.

DIFFICULTY LEVEL

3 Click any adjustment in the Undo History palette to go back to an earlier adjustment.

Note: You can also keep pressing *Ctrl/Cmd+Z to back up in this palette.*

Try This!

Set your Undo History panel for more or fewer adjustment steps or states by clicking Edit, selecting Preferences, and then selecting Performance (see task #14). History states are simply the specific lines of things you have done in the Undo History panel. When you are just doing a few things to the picture, having a lot of history states is not important.

Important!

You will see keyboard commands throughout the book. This is one place where the Mac and PC differs with Photoshop Elements. Ctrl (Control) on the PC is the same as Cmd (or Command) on the Mac. Alt on the PC is the same as Option on the Mac.

Caution!

There is one way you can lose your ability to back up from adjustments. If you make a lot of adjustments to a picture and then save and close it, you lock those adjustments to the picture. Save your photo as you go, but only when you are sure that your adjustments are okay. Later in this book (see task #27), you learn how to make nondestructive adjustments that enable you to close and save an image with those changes intact and still adjustable.

CROP YOUR PHOTOS
for tighter shots

A common problem for photographers is getting too much in a picture. Sometimes this comes from not being able to get close enough to the subject. Other times it results from an excitement about the subject in person that does not translate well to the actual photograph.

Another challenge for photographers is when unwanted details start creeping in to the edges of a picture. That can make the photograph less than its best and even unappealing.

Luckily, Photoshop Elements makes this easy to fix. You can crop your picture down to the essential elements of that image. *Cropping* is simply cutting off parts of the picture to reveal the image previously obscured by extra details. Cropping to strengthen an image and get rid of junk is best done early on in the process. Cropping to a specific size should be done after you have adjusted your photograph optimally.

1. Click the Crop tool in the toolbox at the left.

2. Delete any numbers in the Width, Height, or Resolution boxes.

3. Click a corner of the area you want to keep.

4. Drag your cursor to the opposite corner of the area and release.

5 Click any edge of the crop box.

6 Drag that edge left or right to change the size of the crop box.

7 Click the green check mark to complete the crop.

● The red circle with the diagonal slash removes the crop box.

 # 17

DIFFICULTY LEVEL

● The cropped image now appears in the work area at the same pixel size, but less of the original image appears because of the crop.

Note: You can resize a cropped image to fill the work area by pressing Ctrl/Cmd+0.

TIPS

Try This!

If the Crop tool is not cooperating, you can reset it easily. This is true for all tools. Just above the work area and the toolbox is a toolbar of options for the tool that you are working with. At the far left is a small down-facing arrow. Click it to see options for resetting this tool or all tools. Click Reset Tool.

Try This!

You do not have to use the green check mark to finish your crop. Sometimes it is not efficient to go searching for it. You can use the keyboard and simply press Enter. Or you can use your mouse and double-click inside the box to complete the crop.

Did You Know?

Cropping out the junk early on in the photograph helps as you process the image in Photoshop Elements. Whenever you make any adjustment, Elements looks at the entire picture. Details in the picture that really do not belong can throw off your adjustment.

FIX AND ROTATE
crooked pictures

It is easy to get crooked pictures. Even the pros get them. If you become so excited by the scene or the action within that scene, you might not pay strict attention to the horizon.

Then when you view the photo you took on the computer, you will see that the horizon is crooked. This is not something people viewing the photo typically overlook. If they do, however, the photographer will not miss it and will be disappointed.

Pictures can have crooked verticals, too, but the steps you take to correct them are the same as those for crooked horizontals.

Photoshop Elements makes it easy to straighten a horizon. You can do it a couple of ways. The method you choose depends a lot on the photograph, the degree of crookedness, and your workflow needs.

Use the Straighten Tool

❶ Click the Straighten tool.

❷ Click one side of the crooked horizon.

❸ Drag and release the mouse button when you have created a line across the crooked horizon.

Photoshop Elements straightens the horizon, which makes the picture look crooked in the work area.

❹ Click the Crop tool.

❺ Crop the key part of the photo to remove awkward corners.

❻ Click the green check mark to finish.

Straighten with the Crop Tool

#18

1 Make a narrow crop selection near the horizon using the Crop tool.

2 Position your cursor outside the bounding box until it turns into a curved, two-headed arrow.

3 Click and drag to rotate the bounding box so an edge is parallel to the horizon.

4 Expand the crop box until it covers the correct parts of the photo.

5 Click the green check mark to finish.

TIPS

Try This!

Extreme angles can be fun. Try rotating the crop box to odd and unusual angles and see what happens to the photo. Sometimes you will find interesting, stimulating results. But other times you will get nothing. Keep trying!

Did You Know?

There is a Photoshop joke that applies to Elements, too. How many Photoshop Elements experts does it take to screw in a light bulb? Fifty-one — one person to screw in the bulb and fifty to describe another way to do it. Photoshop and Photoshop Elements are powerful, flexible programs. Use the tools that work for you and ignore people who tell you that you are doing it all wrong. You have to find your own way through Photoshop Elements. It can take some work and time, but it is well worth it when you can work more efficiently.

USE GUIDED EDIT
to help you learn the program

A quick and easy way of working on your images in Photoshop Elements is to use the Guided Edit feature of the program. This feature not only guides you through working on an image, but also gives you a good idea about how Photoshop Elements works.

The Guided Edit feature is truly a guided part of Photoshop Elements. The feature gives you a lot of different options for adjusting the picture, without distracting controls visible. This enables you to focus

on what you need to do to a photograph. Guided Edit does not cover everything in Photoshop Elements but it does provide a good overview of the program. When you click any option in Guided Edit, you go to the control you need as well as instructions on how to use it. Guided Edits contains 19 controls with specific guidance on how to use them. The steps that follow show two of them.

Use Crop Photo

① Click the arrow to the right of the Edit Full tab.

A drop-down menu appears.

② Select Edit Guided.

A new panel appears.

③ Click Crop Photo.

● The Crop tool is selected, a crop box is applied, and instructions appear in the right panel.

④ Click and drag the crop box edges to revise your crop.

⑤ Click Done when you are finished.

Use Enhance Colors

1 Click Enhance Colors.

2 Click Auto if your colors seem off.

3 Drag the Hue slider to change the colors in your photo.

4 Drag the Saturation slider to change the intensity of the colors.

5 Drag the Lightness slider to change the brightness of colors.

6 Click Done when you are finished.

TIPS

Caution!

It is easy to overdo several controls in the Guided Edit panel, creating problems when you want to print your photo or use it in other ways. Be very careful with how strongly you use the brightness and contrast, sharpening, and saturation slide controls so they are not too extreme. There are no warnings about this in the panel.

Try This!

When using the Guided Edit panel, you may find that you inadvertently get adjustments you thought you canceled. That is not a problem. No harm is done, but do not try to correct the adjustment while still in the Guided Edit panel. Go to Edit Full and use your Undo History palette.

Remember This!

Almost all the panels in Guided Edit have a Reset button. This can be a real help. On some of the panels, it is easy to go quickly and overadjust certain controls. It can be hard and confusing to try to readjust them back to zero. Instead, click the Reset button.

SET BLACKS AND WHITES
with Levels

A very important part of any photograph is how the pure black and pure white elements of the image are adjusted. Many cameras do not give a pure black in the image files. Camera designers recognize that black needs vary depending on the type of photography, so they keep this adjustment minimal with the expectation that the photographer should adjust it.

For most pictures, you want a pure black and a pure white somewhere in the picture. Ansel Adams made

this a key point of working in the darkroom, and the needs of a digital color photograph are no different. Without a proper black and white, the picture will not have the best color, the best contrast, or the best overall look. Photographers are often amazed at how much only adjusting the blacks and whites affects the look of the picture. Usually an image requires other adjustments, but this is a good starting point for any photograph.

1 Click Enhance.

2 Select Adjust Lighting.

3 Select Levels.

The Levels dialog box appears.

4 Press the Alt or Option key as you move the black slider under the graph, or *histogram*.

● A threshold screen appears, showing when pure black appears in the photo.

5 Move the slider until at least something black or strongly colored in the image appears.

6 Press Alt or Option as you move the white slider under the graph or histogram.

- A threshold screen appears showing when pure white appears in the photo.

7 Move the slider until at least something shows.

White is very sensitive, so you can stop when colors appear.

8 Click OK when you are done.

The image in the work area now has better color and contrast.

9 Click between Open and Levels in Undo History to see the differences.

Did You Know?

Adjusting the blacks, which refers to all areas of black, is subjective. Some photographers prefer a strong, large area of black within a photograph. Others prefer just a few blacks or only some colors showing up in the threshold screen. Whites are not so subjective. You have to be very careful not to overbrighten them.

Caution!

Not all photos will have blacks. If you try to get blacks in the threshold screen on a foggy-day image, for example, the picture will look harsh and unappealing. Because setting up blacks is subjective, you really have to pay attention to your photograph and its needs, as well as your interpretation of the scene.

More Options!

You may find that some pictures do not seem to have a pure black. All that shows up in the threshold screen is a color. Strongly colored pictures act like this. Do not try to get a pure black, but be sure that you are getting a strong color at least somewhere. That color shows that a channel has been maxed out.

ADJUST YOUR MIDTONES
with Levels

When you set blacks properly, you often find your photo is too dark. It is not actually the whole photo that is too dark, but the *midtones*, the tonalities between black and white.

In fact, these middle tonalities are extremely important to your photograph. They affect the overall brightness of the image, the colors of the photo, and the ability of a viewer to see detail within the picture. Some photographers refer to brightening the

midtones as "opening up" certain tonalities. This is a good way to look at it. You are trying to open up certain parts of the picture so that they can be better seen by the viewer.

This is a subjective adjustment. There is no right or wrong. You have to look at your picture and decide what is the right interpretation for the subject and for how you saw it.

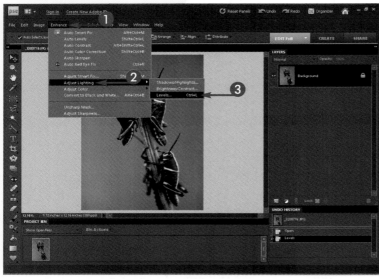

① Click Enhance.

② Select Adjust Lighting.

③ Select Levels.

The Levels dialog box appears.

● Move the middle slider left to brighten the photo.

● Move the middle slider right to darken it.

④ Select and deselect the Preview check box (☐ changes to ☑) and vice versa) to turn the view of the adjustment on and off.

This enables you to better see what is happening in the photo.

⑤ Click OK when you are done.

The image in your work area now has more open midtones and color.

⑥ Click between Open, Levels, and Levels in Undo History to see the differences.

The two Levels make it easy to see the different adjustments.

TIPS

Did You Know?

By separating the adjustments into two variations of Levels, you can more easily see the adjustments and make corrections to them. This step-by-step approach also keeps the steps separate in the Undo History palette. That makes it easier for you to find exactly where a particular adjustment is affecting your picture.

Did You Know?

The graph in the Levels dialog box is called a *histogram*, which is a chart of the brightness values of the pixels in your photograph. As you adjust Levels, you will see small gaps, or white lines, appear in the histogram. Gaps are not a problem. Whether this *combing* of the histogram (as it is called) is a problem depends on what you see happening to the photo. Pay attention to your photo, not arbitrary computer rules.

Important!

The middle slider in the Levels dialog box is a midtones slider, but it affects more than just the very middle tones. As you work in Photoshop Elements, you will start noticing differences between the dark tones with details, middle tones, and bright tones with details.

ADJUST YOUR MIDTONES
with Color Curves

Another way of adjusting midtones is to use Color Curves. Do not be misled by this name. Although the Color Curves adjustment affects color to a degree, it really is a way of affecting tonalities.

The midtones slider in the Levels dialog box affects midtones separately from blacks and whites, with most of the adjustment near the middle tones. You cannot adjust darker tones separately from lighter tones, for example.

Color Curves enables you to separate these adjustments. This gives you more control over the whole range of tones in your picture between the blacks and the whites. This can enable you to open up dark areas, while keeping bright areas at their original darkness, for example. This is important because the camera often captures tonalities in a scene far differently than the way you see them. Color Curves gives you one way of adjusting for that.

① Click Enhance.

② Select Adjust Color.

③ Select Adjust Color Curves.

The Adjust Color Curves dialog box appears.

④ Move the parametric sliders to adjust specific tones in your photo.

Moving the sliders to the right makes tones brighter or contrast higher.

Moving the sliders to the left makes tones darker or contrast less.

● The graph, which shows curves for the adjustments, changes as you move the sliders, but you do not have to know anything about it to use this tool.

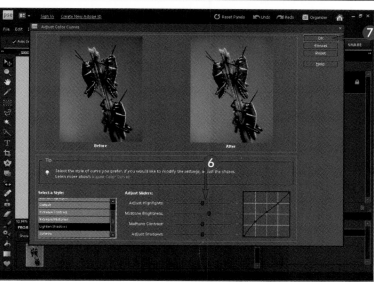

⑤ Select a style at the left side to create adjustments semi-automatically based on the short descriptions that appear in the Tip section.

⑥ Click and adjust the parametric sliders as needed to tweak the style.

⑦ Click OK when you are done.

TIPS

Did You Know?

The sliders in Color Curves are called *parametric* sliders because they affect very specific parameters. They include making highlights brighter or darker, changing the brightness or darkness as well as the contrast of middle tones, and making shadows brighter or darker.

Did You Know?

Color Curves is named after an important adjustment in Photoshop called Curves. As you adjust individual tonalities within a picture, such as highlights separately from shadows, the graph creates curves in its main line; thus the name Curves. The graph represents black at the bottom left and white at the top right.

Try This!

Quick adjustments are better than slow adjustments. Many photographers try to make small adjustments when working in Photoshop Elements. It is easier to see the difference between a good and a bad adjustment if you make the adjustments quickly.

QUICKLY ADJUST
dark shadows and bright highlights

One challenge that consistently faces photographers is a scene that has very bright highlights, or bright areas, and very dark shadows, or dark areas, all within the photo you want to take. The camera then has trouble balancing the brightness throughout the picture. You can see the shadows and highlights just fine, but the camera cannot see them the way you do.

Photoshop Elements can help with this with an adjustment control called Shadows/Highlights. This control searches out the darkest parts of the picture and then adjusts them while limiting the adjustment to those tones. It also finds the brightest parts of the picture and then limits any adjustments to them. It is a very handy control to know about, but you should use it after you adjust blacks and whites as well as midtones.

① Click Enhance.

② Select Adjust Lighting.

③ Select Shadows/Highlights.

The Shadows/Highlights dialog box appears.

④ Click the Lighten Shadows slider and move it to the right to brighten your shadows.

It is important to carefully do these adjustments one at a time to see how they affect the appearance of the photograph.

5 Click the Darken Highlights slider and move it to the right to make your highlights have more color and detail.

6 Click the Midtone Contrast slider and move it to the right or left to make the picture look more natural.

7 Click OK to finish.

The adjusted photo now appears in the central work area of Photoshop Elements.

8 Click different lines, called *states*, of Undo History to see if the adjustments are doing what you want done to your image.

TIPS

Important!

Shadows/Highlights is no magic bullet — it cannot cure all contrast problems in a photograph. Your picture must have detail to work with in the dark and light areas. Shadows/Highlights cannot add detail that the camera did not originally capture.

Did You Know?

Noise creates a sandlike pattern in a picture and can be very annoying. It is rarely noticeable in bright areas with normal exposures. However, it lurks, hidden in the dark areas of the picture. When you brighten dark areas with Shadows/Highlights, noise often becomes more obvious. See task #34 for more on noise.

Caution!

The Shadows/Highlights control is easy to overdo. Watch your picture. Do not simply adjust it so you can see lots of detail in shadows or more detailed highlights. That can result in unnatural-looking images. Make your adjustments so that your picture looks like it was taken on this planet!

CORRECT COLOR
to remove color casts

Color casts are those slight overall colors that seem to permeate the picture. They make neutral colors no longer neutral, and can hurt the appearance of colors so the colors are no longer accurate to the way you saw them. Color casts can cause problems for your subject and your rendition of the scene.

Color casts come from all sorts of things, such as fluorescent lights, blue skies, and improper white balance, which fill a scene with colors, compromising

the look of an image. They used to be a big problem with film, but they are less of one with digital because of the *white balance control*. White balance reduces color casts due to the color of light. This helps, but you can still get a picture with color casts that need to be corrected. In a lot of cameras, auto white balance often gives a slight cold or blue cast to the picture, which can affect skin tones and make them look less attractive.

Remove a Color Cast

1 Click Enhance.

2 Select Adjust Color.

3 Select Remove Color Cast.

The Remove Color Cast dialog box appears.

4 Position your cursor over the photo; the cursor turns into an eyedropper.

5 Click the eyedropper on something that should be neutral in color — a white, gray, or black.

Color casts are removed, but the first click might not work.

6 Click Reset if the colors are not right.

⑦ Keep clicking different tones that should be neutral, clicking Reset if the colors are bad, until you get a good color balance.

⑧ Click OK to finish.

Remove Another Color Cast

This technique works great for people photographs.

① With the Remove Color Cast dialog box open, click different tones in the photo that should be neutral until the color is corrected.

Did You Know?

The Levels dialog box has three eyedroppers on the right side. The black and white eyedroppers affect blacks and whites, but they are heavy-handed and not as effective as using the Levels sliders. The middle eyedropper is, in fact, essentially the same eyedropper as the one used in the Remove Color Cast dialog box.

Did You Know?

You can further adjust the color of skin tones by clicking Adjust Color in the Enhance menu and then clicking Adjust Color for Skin Tone. In this control, you click the skin of a person and Photoshop Elements adjusts the color of the whole picture to make the skin look better. You can further tweak this with some sliders.

Try This!

As you click around in your photograph, you will often find the picture changes to some rather odd colors. That is not a problem because you can click the Reset button. However, you may sometimes find these colors interesting. You can even try clicking colors in the picture just to see what happens.

ENHANCE COLOR
with Hue/Saturation

When photographers discover that they can increase *saturation*, or the color intensity, of the picture with Hue/Saturation, they sometimes take the option too far. The saturation control in Hue/Saturation can very quickly go from enhancing colors to making them look garish.

Although you can adjust the overall colors with Saturation, be careful that you do not overdo it. An adjustment of 10 points or so is usually plenty. The

best way to adjust the saturation in a picture is to adjust individual colors. Your camera does not capture colors equally, so this is a way of getting better color with any photograph.

Hue/Saturation also enables you to adjust the color of the color, or its *hue*. Using the techniques described here, you can, for example, correct the hue of a flower or change the color of someone's jacket by changing the Hue slider.

❶ Click Enhance.

❷ Select Adjust Color.

❸ Select Adjust Hue/Saturation.

The Hue/Saturation dialog box appears.

❹ Click the Master drop-down menu.

❺ Click the first color you want to adjust.

The Master menu now changes to the color you have selected and Photoshop Elements restricts adjustments to that color.

#25

⑥ Click and drag the Saturation slider to the right to increase saturation.

⑦ If needed, click and drag the Hue slider left or right to change the hue of the color.

⑧ Click in the Master drop-down menu again to pick a new color.

⑨ Click and drag the Saturation slider to the right to increase this color's saturation.

⑩ Click and drag the Hue slider if needed.

⑪ Click OK to finish.

TIPS

Try This!

Use your cursor to click in the photo to define color for Hue/Saturation. Once you have selected a color in the Master menu, simply position your cursor over the picture and it turns into an eyedropper. Click the color in the photo and Hue/Saturation will identify that color more precisely.

Did You Know?

Lightness looks like it should be a good control in Hue/Saturation. Unfortunately it is not. It tends to dull colors instead of making them lighter or darker. It is okay to use it in small amounts, but you will find that your colors do not look their best if you try to use it more than that.

Caution!

Be wary of oversaturating your pictures. This control quickly blocks up your colors and makes them look garish if you are not careful. Make your adjustments quickly so that you can see how different the colors are changing and so that your eye does not get used to the gradual color changes.

Use Quick Edit to
WORK FAST

Sometimes you have pictures that you want to work on quickly. You may have promised some prints to a friend or maybe you need to get them ready for presentation. Although all the controls that you have seen in this chapter work well, one challenge is that you have to open up each control individually. That takes time.

In Photoshop Elements Quick Edit, you gain a number of adjustments all in one place that do not need to be opened separately. You cannot control these adjustments as much as the main controls, and they are not as flexible. However, they do work when you need to process pictures quickly. Quick Edit also includes some auto controls. These are also helpful for fast adjustments, but they can take you in the wrong directions for your picture because they are based on formulas instead of what your picture actually looks like.

① Click the arrow to the right of the Edit tab.

② Select Edit Quick.

③ Try clicking Auto in Smart Fix but Smart Fix may or may not help your photo.

④ Tweak Smart Fix if the photo looks almost good enough using the Amount slider.

If you do not like any adjustment, you can press Ctrl/Cmd+Z to undo it.

⑤ Click here to close that Smart Fix panel when you no longer need it.

⑥ Click the Levels and Contrast Auto buttons to see if they help your photo.

If you do not like what these auto functions do, use Ctrl/Cmd+Z to remove their adjustments.

⑦ Adjust the Lighting sliders to make your photo gain the right tonalities.

⑧ Select the check mark to accept the adjustments or the x to cancel them.

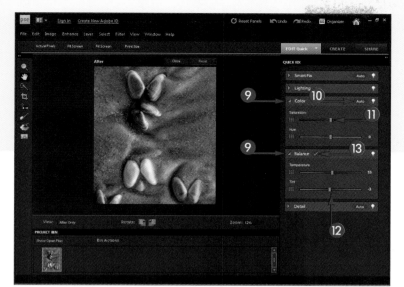

9 Open Color and Balance by clicking the small arrow at the left of the category names.

10 Click the Color Auto button to see if it helps the photo.

11 Adjust the overall color saturation as needed.

12 Adjust Temperature and Tint to affect color casts and the warmth of a photo.

13 Select the check mark to accept any adjustments or the x to cancel them.

26

DIFFICULTY LEVEL

14 Open Detail by clicking here.

15 Click the Magnifier tool in the toolbox at the left.

16 Click the photo to magnify important details.

17 Adjust the Sharpen slider to give an attractive amount of sharpening to your photo.

18 Select the check mark to accept the adjustments or the x to cancel them.

TIPS

Try This!

Try the auto controls, but if they do not work, immediately press Ctrl/Cmd+Z. Auto controls are based on formulas developed by the Photoshop Elements designers. They can work, but they are also somewhat arbitrary because a designer cannot know every person's photos.

Did You Know?

Smart Fix is a useful adjustment when the photo looks a bit off right from the start. For many photos, however, you will find that using Levels and Contrast Auto buttons give better results. You can use Levels alone or add Contrast — this gives you more options and control.

Try This!

You can also use Quick Fix as a starting point for other adjustments. You do not have to make this an either/or question; that is, use Edit Full or Quick Edit. Use Quick Edit to start the process and then refine your adjustments in Edit Full. If you do this, do not use the Sharpen panel area.

Work with RAW Photos in Photoshop Elements

The RAW format available in all digital single lens reflex (dSLR) cameras is a distinct choice from JPEG shooting. Some advanced compact digital cameras also have the RAW format. The RAW and JPEG issue is not an arbitrary quality issue, though some people try to make it so. You can get outstanding results from digital photos whether they are shot in JPEG or RAW.

RAW offers some special benefits that you may want to consider, which made it a good choice for photography. RAW is a proprietary camera file that maximizes the information that comes from your sensor. Every manufacturer has its own version of this type of file. It includes a great deal more tone and color steps than is possible with JPEG. This gives you a lot more flexibility when processing an image before you start to see problems with tones or colors. You can do a lot of things with a JPEG image, but you can do more with a RAW file.

RAW files enable you to dig more detail out of bright areas in a picture, unearth more tones in dark areas, and ensure better gradations when adjusting smooth gradients like skies and out-of-focus sections of a photo.

Top 100

Change images
NONDESTRUCTIVELY

A RAW file is an incomplete photograph. You cannot display such an image file or even print from it without some sort of processing. You can always display a JPEG image in all sorts of programs on your computer, plus you can take a JPEG file straight from the camera and have a print made.

A RAW file must be interpreted by software for it to become a photograph. When this interpretation is done, no changes are ever made to the original RAW file. All adjustments are instructions the computer uses to interpret and process the RAW file. This is called *nondestructive processing* because no pixels from the original file are ever changed. This can be very freeing to you as a photographer because it means you can try almost anything and never damage the original file.

① Click File, and then select Open.

The Open window appears.

② Navigate to a folder with RAW files.

③ Double-click that file to open it.

When you open a RAW file directly in the Editor or from the Organizer, Camera Raw opens, which is Photoshop Elements' RAW software.

● All adjustments are made as instructions from the right side panel as to how to convert the RAW file to a file that can be used in Photoshop Elements.

● The Camera Raw interface offers a lot of adjustments that do not require you to go to a menu.

● The interface also includes a simple toolbox of frequently used tools for photographs.

TIPS

Did You Know?

Whenever you work directly on a photograph in Photoshop Elements, you are working directly on pixels. Those pixels are then changed, which is called *destructive editing*, because the original pixel data is "destroyed" as changes are applied. Camera Raw allows you to make nondestructive changes.

Try This!

You can change the magnification of the displayed photo in Camera Raw by using the magnifier in the toolbox and clicking or dragging the photograph. You can also click the magnification number at the lower left of the photograph to get a drop-down menu of specific magnification sizes.

Did You Know?

JPEG is a processed RAW file. The camera takes the image data coming from the sensor and processes it quickly. The JPEG is a locked-down, processed RAW file. It is good that this file is processed optimally for the particular camera being used, and the file size is much reduced, but it also means the flexibility of the original RAW file is lost.

CROP YOUR PHOTOS
to start your processing

The world does not always cooperate and give you the opportunity to make perfect pictures every time. Sometimes the world does not fit the frame defined by your camera frame. At other times, stuff creeps in along the edges of your picture that really does not belong with your subject.

You should remove these things from your photograph as soon as you start working on an image. This allows you to really focus on the important part of the picture and not be distracted by unimportant things. It also allows you to adjust the picture optimally for what needs to be adjusted and not be influenced by other parts of the original picture.

Cropping is what enables you to keep the details that detract from your image, or the "junk," out of your picture and refine it to the key elements of your subject and scene.

1 Click the Crop tool to select it.

2 Click and drag over the photo to start your crop.

3 Drag the edges and corners of the crop box to make the cropped area larger or smaller.

④ Click inside the photo and drag the crop box to reposition it.

⑤ Press Enter to see the photo as cropped in the work area.

⑥ Click the Crop tool at any time to go back and re-crop the image.

No crop is permanent and can be changed at any time.

Did You Know?

You can re-crop at any time. This is part of the whole idea of the nondestructive processing of an image. Camera Raw remembers how you cropped a particular RAW file, and lets you change that at any time.

More Options!

You can rotate your crop box by simply moving your cursor outside the box so that the cursor changes to a curved double-arrow cursor; then you click and drag to rotate. You can remove or clear your crop by right-clicking the photo to get a menu that includes Clear Crop.

More Options!

You can crop to specific proportions within Camera Raw; however, they are not specific to inches. You can get the specific proportions by either right-clicking the photograph when using the Crop tool to get a context-sensitive menu, or by clicking and holding the Crop tool to get the same menu.

ADJUST BLACKS AND WHITES
to give a photo strength

Chapter 2 described the importance of adjusting blacks and whites in a photograph. This is a very important adjustment to make in Camera Raw because it sets the tonalities for everything else. You have even more flexibility and control when doing this in Camera Raw. You can not only adjust the blacks and whites, but you can also adjust the brightness of the very dark areas and the very bright areas separately.

Blacks can be especially important in giving a photograph and its colors strength. Adjusting blacks is very subjective, but also important. You will find that some photographs need minimal black areas, whereas others need quite large areas of black throughout them. Photoshop Elements helps you out, in a way, by calling this adjustment Blacks. Whites are adjusted, on the other hand, by Exposure. However, you should not use Exposure for adjusting the overall brightness or darkness of the picture.

1 Press the Alt/Opt key and click and drag the Blacks slider.

The blacks threshold screen appears.

● Watch where the pure blacks and maxed-out color channels appear.

Note: *Where anything shows as pure black, it will be a pure black in the photo. Where anything shows as a color, you will be maxing out a certain color in that area.*

2 Adjust the Fill Light slider to give a boost to the darkest areas.

Beware of overadjusting Fill Light so that the photo looks unnatural.

③ Press the Alt/Opt key and click and drag the Exposure (whites) slider.

The whites threshold screen appears.

● Watch where the pure whites and maxed-out color channels appear.

④ Adjust the Recovery slider when highlights look weak and washed out.

Never feel you have to use either the Recovery or Fill Light sliders.

TIPS

Did You Know?
Photographers often refer to the black areas of a photograph as the *blacks* but not because black comes in different brightnesses — it obviously does not. This use of the term *blacks* refers to all the small areas of black scattered throughout the photograph.

Did You Know?
Some people wonder why you need to adjust both the Blacks and Fill Light sliders. They seem to counteract each other. However, such an adjustment gives a different, better look to the dark areas of the picture than occurs if you adjust either one alone or neither one at all.

Important!
Always adjust your blacks first, before using the Fill Light, Exposure, and Recovery sliders. Setting your blacks right away enables you to better see your adjustments for tonality and color. If you adjust Fill Light first, you often find the picture starts to look very gray.

ADJUST MIDTONES
to make tonalities light or dark

In Chapter 2, you also learned about adjusting midtones in a photograph. Once again, this is a very important adjustment to make in Camera Raw. It makes the overall picture lighter or darker. This can help you make the picture look right so that it is neither dark and muddy nor bright and washed out. Adjusting your overall tonalities in Camera Raw enables you to get the optimum results from these tones as well.

You adjust midtones using two sliders in Camera Raw in Photoshop Elements: Brightness and Contrast. Sometimes you will change only the Brightness slider, but just as often you will adjust both. You will rarely adjust only the Contrast slider for most general types of photography, though it can be interesting for certain effects. Brightness and Contrast go well together for adjusting the midtones of your photograph.

① Click and drag the Brightness slider to make the overall photo brighter or darker.

② Adjust the Contrast slider to affect the overall contrast of the photo.

③ Select (☐ changes to ☑) and deselect (☑ changes to ☐) the Preview check box to compare before-and-after adjustments.

④ Readjust the Brightness and Contrast sliders as needed to adapt to each of these controls' changes.

 TIPS

Important!
Adjust your blacks and whites first. Adjusting these tones truly does affect everything else in the photograph. Without a good black in most pictures, colors never look as good and images never print as well. Remember, though, that blacks are subjective and not all photos have them.

Did You Know?
Color is strongly affected by the blacks, whites, and midtones in the picture. Color is not simply a part of your subject; it is subjective and strongly affected by tones all around it. This is why adjusting your blacks, whites, and midtones before trying to control color is so important.

Important!
RAW is no magic bullet that can correct a bad exposure. You need to be especially sure that your bright areas are exposed properly in your image. RAW files have a lot more flexibility in how you can adjust an image, but they cannot bring in detail or tones that the camera and sensor did not originally capture.

CORRECT COLOR
to clean up color casts

Color casts are slight tints of color that appear over the entire photograph. They can be desirable and undesirable. If you are photographing at sunrise or sunset, you want a warm color cast for the photograph. But often, color casts are a problem. They keep you from clearly seeing the colors in a photograph and can put unwanted colors into neutral tones.

You can correct unwanted color casts easily in Camera Raw. It is an easy step where you can quickly make a correction, and then undo or redo it as needed if you do not like it. Because everything in Camera Raw is nondestructive, this is never a problem. By repeatedly making corrections to color to clean up color casts in a photograph, you can learn about color casts and how to better see them.

1 Click the White Balance Tool (the eyedropper) in the toolbox.

2 Move the cursor over the photograph and click something that should be a neutral color.

Camera Raw makes that neutral color neutral and removes a color cast.

③ Try clicking another location to see if you get a better color.

When the color looks good, you are done.

If the color looks really bad, press Ctrl/Cmd+Z to undo the adjustment.

④ Change the Temperature and Tint sliders to further adjust the color.

Try This!

You can use Camera Raw's white balance settings to affect your photograph. Click the White Balance down arrow and you get a drop-down menu of white balance settings. Click any one to see what it does to a photo and what the image looks like. These are not the same as settings on your camera. They are Adobe interpretations of the white balance settings.

Did You Know?

The white balance settings in Camera Raw look like the settings on a camera. You might think they are the same settings and you use them the same way. Although they are similar, these settings represent Adobe colors based on how Adobe engineers deal with colors for the settings.

Important!

RAW is sort of a magic bullet when it comes to white balance. You can change your white balance settings as much as you want without any harm to the picture, plus you can adjust a picture that is way out of balance quite easily. Still it is best to select a white balance setting in your camera because this will make your colors more consistent.

USE VIBRANCE AND CLARITY
to intensify images

Vibrance and Clarity are two relatively new adjustments for Camera Raw in Photoshop Elements. Vibrance affects color. This control can increase or decrease the intensity of a color. It is like Saturation, an older tool that is much more heavy-handed, but it does not oversaturate colors as easily. Vibrance also affects less-saturated colors more than Saturation does and has a strong effect on skies.

Clarity adjusts the contrast of midtones. It is a visual effect that is hard to explain. A way to see how it affects an image is to drag the slider all the way to the right, look at the effects on the picture, and then drag the slider all the way to the left and view those effects. Then move the slider in the direction that seems best for your picture, though not to one of the extremes.

① For an image with interesting midtone detail, move the Clarity slider 20 to 40 points to the right.

Clarity can make a subject look too harsh if it is overdone.

② To give your photo a little boost in color, move the Vibrance slider 20 to 35 points to the right.

74

③ If the color looks good but seems to pick up a color cast, try adjusting the Temperature and Tint sliders.

Be wary of using the Saturation slider because it is easy to overdo its effects.

④ If you feel the photo still needs more lively colors, try using the Saturation slider up to about 12 points.

Try This!

Whenever you want to reset a slider in Camera Raw, double-click the slider adjustment "knob." This immediately resets that slider to its default. It can be a good way of seeing exactly what your adjustment is doing to a picture. Just remember what your setting is before you double-click.

Did You Know?

Some people confuse Clarity with sharpness. Clarity is not sharpness, but a way of affecting a very specific contrast within your picture — the contrast of midtones. This can make a picture look like it is being sharpened, but Clarity is not as refined an adjustment as sharpening.

Attention!

Portraits and increased Clarity do not always go well together. Clarity intensifies pores, wrinkles, and defects in a person's skin, which is not always very flattering. In fact, portraits sometimes look better if Clarity is decreased so that skin texture is not as pronounced.

SHARPEN PHOTOS
with precision

Traditionally, the standard recommendation for sharpening has been to sharpen your image at the very end of your processing. This is because some of the strong adjustments to a photograph can affect sharpening. However, the sharpening tools in Photoshop Elements Camera Raw offer new algorithms that work well. In addition, you are doing most of your strong adjustments in Camera Raw, so it is appropriate to do sharpening here. Finally, Camera Raw smartly applies sharpening at the right time in the processing process.

With experience, you might find certain photographs require much more adjustment in Photoshop Elements itself. When that happens, you may decide to do sharpening at the end of all your adjustments. Photoshop Elements has good sharpening tools, so it is okay to do sharpening here instead of in Camera Raw. But if Camera Raw becomes an important part of your workflow, you will do most of your sharpening in it.

① Click the Detail tab in the adjustment panel on the right.

This opens the Sharpening and Noise Reduction adjustments.

② Click 100% in the magnification menu at the lower left so that you can better see the sharpening effects.

③ Move the Amount slider to the right until the image starts to look sharp, but no more.

④ Try moving the Radius slider a little to the right to see if it helps your photo.

⑤ Use the Detail slider to help bring out small detail in the photograph.

⑥ Use the Masking slider to limit your sharpening to the strongest edges.

⑦ Press Alt/Opt to see the mask where white allows the sharpening and black blocks it.

Masking can be very important when your subject is sharp and the background is out of focus.

TIPS

Did You Know?

Amount controls the intensity of the sharpening. Radius affects how far sharpening is applied around pixel-sized detail. Detail modifies how strongly Radius interacts with Amount on details. Masking changes where sharpening is applied by blocking it from less-detailed areas.

Try This!

Press and hold the Alt/Option key as you adjust any of the Sharpening controls and the image changes to a black-and-white rendition of how that control is affecting the picture. Some photographers find it easier to see the sharpening effects this way because color can be distracting.

Caution!

Avoid oversharpening your photos. Sharpening is not meant to make a blurry picture sharp. You need to get the best sharpness possible when you take the picture. Increasing the sharpening controls too much can make your picture look harsh and unappealing.

CONTROL NOISE
in your photo

Noise is inherently a part of digital photography. The latest cameras control noise extremely well, especially with proper exposure. However, every camera has its own noise characteristics for an image file. Cameras with smaller image sensors have more noise, higher ISOs increase noise, and underexposure of a scene also increases noise in the final picture. All this makes noise more apparent as you sharpen the photo.

This is why Camera Raw includes Noise Reduction in the Detail tab along with Sharpening. You can affect two types of noise — the sandlike pattern of luminance noise and the color pattern of color noise. Noise Reduction works well for average amounts of noise in standard photographs. However, it does not work that well for strong or severe noise in an image. For that, you need special software designed specifically for noise reduction.

① Click 100% to 200% in the magnification menu at the lower left so that you can see noise more clearly.

② Press the spacebar to get the Hand tool and move the photo to find a dark, smooth area that shows noise.

③ Move the Luminance slider to the right until the noise starts to smooth out, but no more.

You can move the Color slider to the right if you see colored speckles that represent color noise.

④ Move the Color slider to the left from the default setting if, as in this example, there is no color noise present.

● Avoid high amounts of Luminance or Color noise reduction, as shown here, because it can adversely affect the small detail and color in your photo.

TIPS

Did You Know?

Dark areas show noise more quickly than any other parts of a photograph when they are brightened. This is why you should avoid underexposing your pictures, forcing you to brighten dark areas, thereby increasing noise.

Caution!

Noise is essentially tiny details in your picture. Reducing noise can also reduce other tiny details, so you need to be careful about how strongly you use the Noise Reduction sliders. The Color slider can also affect small but important color detail in your picture.

Check It Out!

When noise starts to become problematic in a photograph, you need to use other methods of noise reduction than what is available in Camera Raw. Dfine from Nik Software (www.niksoftware.com) or Noiseware from Imagenomic (www.imagenomic.com) are two programs that work well with Photoshop Elements. See task #88 for more about Dfine.

Apply adjustments to
MULTIPLE PHOTOS

Often, you will photograph a subject or scene a variety of ways. Yet the exposure and the light is basically the same among all these shots. It would take a lot of time to process each picture individually, but you do not have to. Camera Raw in Photoshop Elements allows you to apply multiple adjustments to photographs at the same time. This is a big timesaver. This is also a benefit for photographers

who shoot certain subjects in standardized ways, such as portraits under a specific lighting setup. Portrait photographers, especially, often take a lot of pictures of a single subject or several subjects with few changes in exposure or lighting. Processing all the pictures would be a pain if you could not do something to adjust all of them very quickly.

① Press Ctrl/Cmd+click to select several similar RAW images in Organizer that need the same sorts of adjustments.

② Click the arrow at the right of the Fix tab.

③ Select Full Photo Edit to move the images to Camera Raw.

● Camera Raw opens, now with a series of photos on the left.

④ Click the photo that can be adjusted most easily first.

That photo appears in the work area.

⑤ Click Select All to select the whole group of photos.

6 Adjust the work area photo as best you can.

● Adjustments are automatically applied to the other photos, as well.

7 Click any individual photo.

8 Refine the adjustments on that photo as needed.

● Adjustments are only applied to this photo.

TIPS

Try This!

You can use this technique when you want to change one or two adjustments for your group of pictures and not have everything changed as you go. First make only the specific adjustments you want to use across multiple pictures and do them for the selected group of pictures. Then go in and do the normal adjustments to individual pictures as needed.

Check It Out!

As you make adjustments, an icon (▤) appears at the lower right-hand corner of your image that tells you adjustments have been made. This helps you keep track of which images have been adjusted if you are adjusting a group of photos one at a time.

Warning!

As you adjust your photographs in Camera Raw, you may notice a small yellow triangle with an exclamation point in it in the upper right-hand corner of the images. This is a warning icon, but not something you have to worry about. It indicates your computer is working on processing these images for display.

MOVE YOUR PICTURE
to Photoshop Elements

Once you are done working on your image in Camera Raw, you need to move your picture to the Photoshop Elements Editor. Camera Raw is a separate program from Photoshop Elements, so you have to get your pictures out of that program and loaded into Editor.

Because everything you do in Camera Raw is just instructions on how to process and convert the image from the RAW file to an actual picture file, that

conversion must occur for you to work on the image outside of Camera Raw. These instructions are also saved as a separate, companion file to your RAW file so that if you open that RAW file again in Camera Raw, all your adjustments are still there. Because the RAW file cannot be changed, only converted, no adjustments are actually applied to any of the data in that file.

1 Click the Depth pop-up menu.

2 Choose 8 Bits/Channel.

You can save your image converted to a DNG file, which is a special Adobe RAW file that Adobe promises to always support.

3 Click Save Image.

The Save Options dialog box appears.

4 Choose a destination.

5 Name your file.

6 Click Save.

You can open your image directly into Photoshop Elements.

⑦ Click Open Image.

● The photo opens into Photoshop Elements, converted from the RAW file based on the adjustments you made in Camera Raw.

TIPS

Did You Know?

Bit depth represents how much processing flexibility you have in an image file. You are processing in Camera Raw at the maximum capability of 16-bit. Unless you are planning to do a lot of processing in Photoshop Elements, you can easily use the smaller 8-bit file there.

More Options!

When using Save As, you can choose a number of possibilities, including PSD for processing later in Photoshop Elements, JPEG for Web use or small archival files, TIFF for use with publications, and DNG, Adobe's general purpose RAW file.

Try This!

If you find you consistently adjust your images a certain way, you can reset Camera Raw defaults so these adjustments are always done to an image as soon as it opens. Make those adjustments to a file and then click the icon with three lines (▤). Choose Save New Camera Raw Defaults from the menu that appears.

Choose Local Control Features

The real world is often quite different from the photograph that your camera captures. This is not your fault or the camera's; it is simply a reflection of the fact that the camera sees the world differently than people do. One very common problem is that the camera makes certain things brighter or darker in proportion to other objects in the scene compared to the way that you actually see them. Another problem is that color relationships are often recorded differently compared to the way people see them.

A way to correct these problems is to isolate them in a photograph so you can adjust them separately from the rest of the image. This is called *local control* as compared to overall or global control over the whole image. This technique was common when photographers spent time in the traditional darkroom. It used to be hard to do with color photography, but the computer changed that. With Photoshop Elements, you have the ability to select and isolate very specific parts of the picture and then make corrections to that isolated area so that no other parts of the picture are affected. That is a very important capability for a photographer.

Top 100

CREATE AND USE
a Selection

Selections are a key way of isolating a part of the picture for adjustment separate from the rest. A selection is a little bit like building a fence. If you build a fence in the middle of a field and put all the cows in there, they eat the grass there and nowhere else. If you create a selection in the middle of the picture, any adjustments that you make occur inside that selection and nowhere else.

Photoshop Elements offers a number of ways to create selections, and you will learn them in this chapter. The reason for the choice of selections is to make selections easier, more effective, and more precise for the specific needs of individual pictures. In this task, you learn what a selection can do, how it works, and how it combines with adjustments to control where an adjustment occurs.

① Open a photo in the Editor by going to File and then Open and selecting a file for processing.

② Click the Rectangular Marquee tool in the toolbox.

③ Click and drag a rectangular selection inside your picture.

④ Click Enhance, select Adjust Lighting, and then select Levels to open the Levels dialog box.

⑤ Make an extreme adjustment in the Levels dialog box to see the effect.

⑥ Click Cancel.

⑦ Click Enhance, select Adjust Color, and then select Adjust Hue/Saturation to open the Hue/Saturation dialog box.

⑧ Select the Colorize check box (☐ changes to ☑).

⑨ Make an extreme adjustment with Hue and Saturation so that you can see the effect.

⑩ Click Cancel.

TIPS

Try This!

As you experiment with new controls in Photoshop Elements, you will typically close one file and open another to see the effects on varied subjects. You can always close and open images from the File menu. You can also close any open photo by clicking the small X in the image area tab that sits above the image.

Change It!

Once you have a selection, you can easily get rid of it and start a new selection at any time. Press Ctrl/Cmd+D to deselect your selection. You can also click your cursor outside of a selection to deselect as well, as long as you are still using a selection tool.

Did You Know?

Colorize is an interesting part of Hue/Saturation because it does not simply change colors in a picture — it adds colors to a picture. When you select that check box, the adjustment adds whatever color is chosen in the Hue area to the photograph. You can then adjust the intensity of this color using the Saturation slider.

USE MARQUEE TOOLS
for specific shapes

The rectangular and elliptical selection tools in the toolbox are called the Marquee selection tools. They both sit in the same place at the upper-left side of the toolbox. By default, the Rectangular Marquee tool is visible. The Elliptical Marquee tool is underneath the rectangle. To access the elliptical tool, click and hold the Rectangular Marquee tool until a small menu appears that shows both tools. You then select the one you want.

The rectangular and elliptical tools provide exactly what you expect, rectangle and ellipse shapes. They are great to experiment with when you are learning selections because they are so obvious. Their shapes are so specific, however, that most photographers use them infrequently because most photographs do not have these specific shapes. Still, when you do need them, they give you specific, precise shapes in a hurry.

Use the Rectangular Marquee Tool

❶ Click the Rectangular Marquee tool in the toolbox.

❷ Click and drag a selection around an area that works with the shape.

❸ Choose an adjustment appropriate for the selected area inside your photograph.

❹ Make the adjustment.

In this example, the blacks and whites are strongly adjusted with the appropriate sliders in Levels.

The adjustment only occurs inside the selected area.

❺ Click OK.

Use the Elliptical Marquee Tool

1 Click the Elliptical Marquee tool in the toolbox.

2 Click and drag a selection around an area that works with the shape.

The elliptical tool takes some practice getting used to.

Experiment with it to see how it might work for you.

#38

DIFFICULTY LEVEL

3 Open an adjustment appropriate for the selected area inside your photograph.

4 Make the adjustment.

5 Click OK.

TIPS

More Options!

The Marquee tools also do the square and circle selections. To get a square, choose the Rectangular Marquee tool and press and hold the Shift key as you make the selection. To create a circular selection, choose the Elliptical Marquee tool and press and hold the Shift key again as you make the selection.

Try This!

Once you have created a selection, you can move it to a better place in your photograph as needed. Simply click in the selection area and hold down the mouse button. Then drag the selection to a new area. You can also move your selection with the arrow keys.

More Options!

If you look closely, you notice that a lot of the tools in the toolbox have a little black triangle to the bottom right of the icon. This indicates that more tools are available than what is showing. Clicking and holding the icon reveals a stack of tools.

USE LASSO TOOLS
to follow picture elements

The Rectangular and Elliptical Marquee tools are pretty restrictive as to what they can do in a photograph. Most photographs do not have such specific shapes. Photoshop Elements gives you additional freehand tools such as the Lasso, the Polygonal Lasso, and the Magnetic Lasso tools for selecting in any shape.

The Polygonal Lasso is probably the easiest to use for most photographers. You simply click the place to start and then move your cursor along a selection,

clicking as you go to anchor the selection. You complete the selection by clicking the beginning point or double-clicking anywhere. The Magnetic Lasso is an automated lasso that finds edges for you. If you have a strong edge where your selection needs to be, you start this tool near that edge and it finds the edge for you. The Lasso works totally freehand, going wherever your cursor goes, but it can be hard to control without a lot of practice.

① Click and hold the Lasso tool in the toolbox.

② Select Polygonal Lasso Tool.

③ Click at one edge where you want to make a selection.

④ Move the cursor along the edge, clicking regularly to anchor the selection edge.

● The selection edge follows your cursor.

⑤ Click and move your cursor around the area that you want to select.

⑥ Finish the selection by clicking where you started.

The cursor adds a small o at the cursor's lower right when it is over the starting point.

DIFFICULTY LEVEL

⑦ Choose an adjustment appropriate for the selected area inside your photograph.

⑧ Make the adjustment.

In this example, the bird's body has been lightened.

⑨ Click OK.

The adjustment is now made only inside the selected area.

TIPS

Important!

Selections take practice. When you first start using selections, you may find it frustrating to make your selections go exactly where you want them. With practice, you get much better. You can also find ideas in the rest of this chapter that can help you create selections easier.

Try This!

The Magnetic Lasso is very useful when you have a picture in which, for example, your subject contrasts strongly against a simple background. The Magnetic Lasso looks for contrasting edges and finds them for you. This makes selection easy as long as you have those edges.

More Options!

Because the Polygonal Lasso goes in a straight line from click to click, you might think it is not useful for curves. In fact, this tool is actually good for curves because it is easy to control: Just move your cursor in short distances as you click around a curve.

USE AUTOMATED TOOLS
for easy selections

Photoshop Elements offers a diversity of selection tools so that you have options for matching a tool with the selection challenge in a photograph. Adobe has even added some automated tools that help you find edges and create selections quickly for certain types of pictures. One of them, the Magnetic Lasso, was described in the previous task.

Three more very useful automated selection tools are the Magic Wand, the Selection Brush, and the Quick

Selection tool. The Magic Wand is used for areas that have a consistent tone or color. Click that area and the Magic Wand finds all pixels similar to the color and tone where you clicked. The Selection Brush enables you literally to paint a selection in the picture by brushing your cursor over an area. The Quick Selection tool is sort of in between. You use it to brush through an area; it finds additional pixels that match that area in tone and color.

① Click the Magic Wand in the toolbox.

② Click in an even-toned, colored area to begin the selection.

A selection is created based on the color and tone where you click.

③ Change the Tolerance for the tool if the selection goes too far or does not go far enough.

④ Click the tool once in an unselected area or twice if those areas are small; click once to remove the old selection, and click once again to create a new selection.

You may also find that it helps to click in different places.

5 Click and hold on the tool below the Magic Wand.

6 Click the Selection Brush tool.

40

DIFFICULTY LEVEL

7 Paint over an area you want to select using the Selection Brush.

8 Change the size if the brush is too big or small for the area.

TIPS

More Options!
The Contiguous check box for the Magic Wand is a very useful. When it is selected (☑), the selection captures only contiguous, or connected, areas. When it is deselected (☐), the selection looks for any places in your photograph that have the same colors and tone, connected or not.

More Options!
The Tolerance setting for the Magic Wand is an important option. It tells the tool how to look at tones and colors within the picture to make the selection. Set it lower to restrict your selection, and higher to make it find more parts of the picture.

Save It!
Once you have a good selection, you may want to keep it so that you can go back to the selection later. You can save that selection. Click the Select menu and select Save Selection. Type a name for the selection, keep New Selection selected, and click OK.

EXPAND OR CONTRACT
your selection

After you create a selection, you often find that it is not quite right. That is normal. Making a perfect selection in one try can be difficult. Luckily, Photoshop Elements has features that enable you to refine a selection and make it do what you want it to do. You can easily add to a selection or subtract from a selection as needed.

This is very important because it makes selecting easier. You do not have to worry about making a

selection perfect right from the start. In fact, making your first selection very quickly and then refining that selection to the final area is often easier and faster than trying to do it exactly right as you go. No matter what you do, you will often find little jags, corners, and other odd shapes easier to deal with after you have done your first selection work.

1 Click the Zoom tool in the toolbox.

Note: It usually helps to magnify the selected area so you can better see the edges.

2 Click and drag the magnifier around the area to magnify it.

3 Click the Selection Brush in the toolbox.

4 Click here.

A size slider appears.

5 Change the brush to a size appropriate to the areas you need to select.

6 Click and drag to brush a selection.

41

⑦ Hold down the Alt/Opt key and then click and drag the Brush tool to remove part of a selection.

Remove all excess selection areas.

⑧ Use a brush sized appropriately to add specific areas to a selection.

Refine your selection by adding or subtracting to it. You can repeatedly go back and forth between the default add function and the subtract function of the brush. Remember that the brush automatically adds to a selection unless you press and hold the Alt/Opt key.

TIPS

Try It!
The Lasso tool is ideal for adding and subtracting from a selection. It can be hard to use when trying to make a large selection, but for little adjustments and selection refinements, it works well. Press and hold the Alt/Opt key to remove part of a selection and hold down the Shift key to add to a selection when using the Lasso tool.

More Options!
You might have noticed that your cursor changes when it goes over the word Size in the options bar. Your cursor becomes activated and you can simply click Size and drag left and right to make the brush size smaller or larger respectively. Many numerical options in Photoshop Elements work this way.

Try This!
You can make your brush size larger or smaller very quickly by using the keyboard. To the right of the letter P are the bracket keys, [and]. Press the [and the brush gets smaller. Press the] and the brush gets larger. You will find this is very handy for sizing your brush to the perfect size.

SELECT WHAT IS EASY
and invert

Photographs can be challenging at times. You want to make an adjustment to a very specific part of the picture, but selecting that area is difficult.

One way to deal with this is to look at your picture carefully before you start making a selection. You may discover that it is easier to select something beside your subject or another area. This would not help you if it were all you could do, because you do

not really want to select that area. However, Photoshop Elements enables you to make a selection and then invert it or flip it over so that what was selected is now unselected and what was unselected is now selected. Often when you look at a picture you can find easier ways of making a selection than simply creating an outline around it.

Note: Skies are often very easy to select with the Magic Wand and can be used to start a selection around a complex shape.

1 Click the Magic Wand in the toolbox.

2 Deselect the Contiguous check box (☑ changes to ☐).

This enables Magic Wand to select similar areas throughout the photo, even when they are not connected.

3 Click the sky to begin the selection.

4 Press the Shift key and click the sky again to add to the selection.

5 Click Select.

6 Choose Inverse.

7 Open an adjustment dialog box
based on what you need to
change, such as Levels.

8 Make an adjustment.

● The adjustment applies to the
area you originally wanted to
work on, but not to the sky.

TIPS

More Options!

Remember that you do not have to
do a complete selection in one try.
You can use this technique to do
the best you can, such as selecting
the sky and inverting the selection.
Then you can add to that selection
or subtract from it using other
selection tools. Simply press and
hold the Shift key while selecting to
add, or the Alt/Opt key to subtract.

Try It!

Sometimes the outline around your
selection can be distracting.
Pressing Ctrl/Cmd+H temporarily
hides the selection outline, yet it is
still there. Press Ctrl/Cmd+H again
and the selection outline reappears.
Do not forget that you used this
command or you will get frustrated
that controls are not working right
because of a "hidden" selection.

Put It Together!

Use whatever selection tools
make it easiest to get your
selection started. Then use the
Inverse command as well as
adding to and subtracting from a
selection to refine your selection
as needed. Using multiple tools
like this helps a lot in getting
better selections.

BLEND EDGES
by feathering

Selections create a very hard edge between the selected and unselected areas, a hard edge that is really not normal in a photograph. Magnify any photograph and you rarely see a razor-sharp edge anywhere. This is because of the way light works as well as how things go in and out of focus in an image. Using an unmodified selection this way can look very unnatural in the picture.

Photoshop Elements gives you the opportunity to make this edge blend in. This is called *feathering*. Feathering has to be adjusted for every selection, because how much of a blend is needed depends entirely on the subject in the photograph. This is why it is best to do feathering after you have made a selection, because if you do not like the effect, you simply undo it and try another amount. The selection remains unchanged.

① Use the Zoom tool to magnify an image with a selection so you can see the edge clearly.

② Open an adjustment control appropriate to your photo to affect something in a selection.

③ Make a strong adjustment so that the difference between selected and unselected areas is extreme.

● Note the hard edge between adjusted and unadjusted areas.

Pressing Ctrl/Cmd+H hides and unhides the selection outline to make the edge easier to see.

④ Click Cancel.

The image now appears with the selection and no adjustment.

⑤ Click Select.

⑥ Choose Feather.

The Feather Selection dialog box opens.

⑦ Type a moderate number for Feather Radius such as 25.

Note: *The amount of Radius is relative and will be "large," "moderate," or "small" based on the size of the selection and the pixel size of the photo.*

⑧ Click OK.

⑨ Open an adjustment dialog box, the same one you did before appropriate to your image.

⑩ Make a strong adjustment now that really changes the selected area.

● Note how the adjustment now blends nicely in the photo.

TIPS

More Options!

To get a feathered edge on your selection when using the Selection Brush, choose a soft-edge brush. After selecting the Selection Brush, right-click the photograph to get choices for brush sizes. You can see the difference between a soft- and hard-edge brush by the softness or hardness of the little circles.

Did You Know?

When you choose an adjustment control after making a selection, the dialog box that opens shows you what is happening only inside the selection. For example, the Levels dialog box shows something distinctly different for the selection than if you use Levels for the entire picture. The control is affecting only that selected area.

Change It!

Feathering values affect how far a selection blends between the selected and unselected areas. If the photograph has fairly sharp edges as in the example, you typically use a low number, such as one between 5 and 10. If there is no sharp edge or you want the blend to cross a wider part of the picture, use a high number, such as one between 60 and 100.

USE SELECTIONS FOR
traditional edge darkening

Photographers working in the traditional darkroom typically add a little bit of darkness along the edges of their pictures. This is called *burning in* the edges because of the way light is used to darken these edges. Ansel Adams considered this a critical part of working on an image in the darkroom. He felt that the viewer's eye had a tendency to drift off a photograph because of the surroundings. Darkening the edge would help keep the viewer's eye focused on the photograph.

You can do this using a selection. How much you darken an edge is subjective and depends on your photograph. You do not want to make the effect too obvious, and you want to keep a good blend across the edge between the darkening and the rest of the photograph. Once you try this, you will discover that it gives your picture a livelier look.

① Choose the Lasso tool from the toolbox.

② Draw a rough outline around the photograph, in from the edges but away from your main subject.

③ Open the Feather Selection control from the Select menu.

④ Type a large number for Feather Radius, such as one between 140 and 200.

⑤ Click OK.

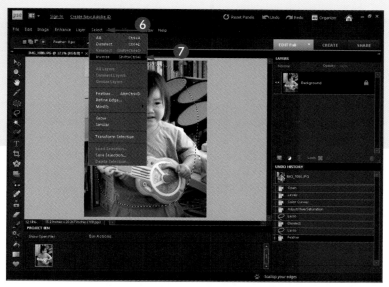

The selection outline smoothes its shape, though you cannot see the actual feathering yet.

6 Click Select.

7 Select Inverse.

DIFFICULTY LEVEL

The selection is now along the outside edges of the image.

8 Click Enhance, select Adjust Lighting, and then select Brightness/Contrast to open the Brightness/Contrast dialog box.

9 Click and drag the Brightness slider to the left to darken the outside edges of the photograph.

Pressing Ctrl/Cmd+H hides the selection outline to make the edge easier to see.

10 Select and deselect the Preview check box to see how the effect works (☐ changes to ☑) and vice versa.

 TIPS

Attention!

Brightness/Contrast seems like it would be a good all-around adjustment for photographers. It is not. Its use should be restricted to special purposes such as darkening the outside edges of a photograph. It is a rather blunt-edged instrument for most adjustments in a photograph.

Test It!

Experiment with feathering. Feathering is not some absolute thing for which you can pick an arbitrary number and be done with it. The same feathering numbers can look perfect on one photograph and awful on another. It is okay to try a number, do the adjustment, undo the effect if you dislike it, and try again.

Did You Know?

Ansel Adams was a master landscape photographer who spent a lot of time in a traditional darkroom. He felt that the original exposure was only an approximation of what he really saw at the scene. He used his time in the darkroom to bring out the best in his images so that the scene was interpreted more closely to the way he actually saw it.

USE THE SMART BRUSH
for specific area fixes

Beginning with Photoshop Elements 7, Adobe has introduced a special brush that enables you to brush on local adjustments in a photograph. The Smart Brush combines the Selection Brush with a whole range of preset adjustments that you choose and then use on your photograph. These adjustments specifically define how such things as color, contrast, and special effects are applied to your photograph in restricted areas. They are easy to use, and are well

worth experimenting with to see what all the presets can do for your photographs. Some photographers find all of the presets very useful, whereas others use only a limited group.

Although you do not have to know anything about layers or layer masks to use the Smart Brush, this tool uses layers and layer masks for its effects. You will see a new layer appear in the Layers palette when you use the brush.

① Choose the Smart Brush from the toolbox.

② Click the Preset selector.

③ Choose the preset appropriate for your photo's needs.

In this example, the Greenery preset was selected to intensify the green leaves of the wood sorrel and make them stand out more.

④ Change the size of your brush with the bracket keys ([ ) and ( ]) until it is sized correctly for the space.

⑤ Brush the preset change onto the photo over the area that needs the adjustment.

6 Add or subtract from the changed area with the plus and minus brushes.

Examine the change; if it is good, continue working on the photo.

7 Click the first Smart Brush icon to start a new Smart Brush adjustment using the same adjustments.

This enables you to do the same adjustment, but at different locations and with different amounts.

8 Click the red Smart Brush icon (◼) to refine the adjustment.

Note: The Smart Brush working icons change color as you add Smart Brush adjustments.

● The Adjustments panel opens that automatically gives you the correct adjustment controls. If it does not open, use the Window menu and select Adjustments.

9 Change the adjustment to refine the work that the Smart Brush did.

This adjustment is up to you and will vary depending on the type of brush you chose.

In this image, the hue of the leaves was slightly changed.

TIPS

Did You Know?

The Smart Brush is a very handy tool because you can reopen its adjustment and readjust the controls as much as you want. No harm will come to your picture when you do this, which makes it a great tool to experiment with. Just click the appropriate Smart Brush working icon for each adjustment.

Did You Know?

Layers are a way of working with a photograph to keep adjustments separate from one another. They also enable you to make temporary adjustments to a picture that you can adjust again and again without harming the picture. You will learn more about layers in the next chapter.

Test It!

To totally remove a Smart Brush adjustment, you need to remove the layer on which the adjustment was made. That is easy to do. Simply go to the Layers palette, click the layer named for the adjustment you want to remove, and then drag it to the Trash Can icon below the layers. This is explained in more detail in the next chapter.

Create Adjustment Layers for Nondestructive Changes

Photoshop Elements is pixel-editing software, designed to work with the pixels of a digital image. This is what you have been doing in the book so far except for your work with the Smart Brush in task #45. One problem with working directly on the pixels of an image is that every time they are changed, there is the potential for the loss of image quality as the pixel data changes. The pixels cannot gain more information, but they can lose it.

You can work on your image without changing any pixels by using adjustment layers and layer masks. Adjustment layers give you a huge range of flexibility and power that you do not

get when working directly on the pixels of an image. The interface for Photoshop Elements 8 and adjustment layers has changed. These controls are now opened as a panel in the panel bin.

Adjustment layers are a lot like filters on the camera. If you put a filter on your lens, the scene does not change, but it does look different coming through the lens and onto your sensor. An adjustment layer does something very similar, changing how the pixels of a photograph appear yet not actually changing any pixel in the underlying picture.

Top 100

Understand
HOW LAYERS WORK

Step away from Photoshop Elements for a minute and you will discover you already know quite a bit about layers. Your keyboard on your desk is a layer. A book is made up of many layers of pages. Why is it that you cannot see the filling of a pie that has a thick top crust? Because that crust is a layer.

This is important to keep in mind because layers in Photoshop Elements act the same way. They are simply a stack of digital things, from adjustment

layers to actual photographs. The stack has a top and a bottom, the top covers up everything underneath it, and you examine a stack from top to bottom. Further, if you put a piece of green cellophane over a real-world stack of anything, such as a pile of papers, everything looks green, even though nothing has actually changed color. The same thing happens with Photoshop Elements.

- This photo looks perfectly normal, except that what you are seeing is the result of layers, which are shown in the Layers panel.

- The original photo is at the bottom, but you are not seeing that.

- A solid sky layer blocks any view of the original photo, just as if you painted blue on a piece of plastic over a photo.

  Just like the paint on plastic, the original photo is still there, unharmed.

- The building has been copied to a new layer.

- The tree leaves have also been copied to a new layer.

- Even though these layers have separate picture elements, they combine visually to look exactly like the original photo.

- The sky has been moved up in the layer stack, now blocking the view of the building.

- The building is still there, but because layers affect what is underneath them, the sky keeps the building hidden.

- The tree leaves still show up because they are higher in the layer stack.

  Layers always work so that higher layers affect layers underneath them.

  Because layers separate parts of a photo, you can easily change one part without affecting another.

- Now the photo looks just like building and sky.

- The original photo is still there, untouched.

- The building has been moved to the top of the layer stack.

- The tree leaves have been moved to below the solid sky, so the sky hides the tree.

TIPS

Did You Know?

If for any reason you discover that your panels are not appearing, select the Window menu. It has a list of items to display in the Photoshop Elements interface. You can turn any of them on or off by clicking the name of the panel.

Try This!

You can easily move layers up and down in the Layers panel. Click a layer and drag it to a new position. Photoshop Elements automatically opens a space for it and shifts the other layers to make room for it.

Did You Know?

The biggest benefit of layers is it gives you the ability to isolate parts of a photo. This enables you to work separately on those parts, and having layers gives you more options for blending separate elements in different layers.

Adjustment layers include many of the adjustment controls that you have seen so far in the book. An adjustment layer even shows the same controls, such as the Levels adjustment — the dialog box for Levels has identical controls to the Levels panel for an adjustment layer.

Yet using an adjustment layer is considerably different from adjusting on the photograph. These special layers are basically instructions. As you make an adjustment, the underlying picture appears to change, yet it really does not. What changes is the view through the adjustment layer. That means you can adjust and readjust the controls in an adjustment layer because the underlying picture never changes. This also means that the adjustments are nondestructive because pixels are not damaged in any way. In this task you try an adjustment layer to see how these layers work.

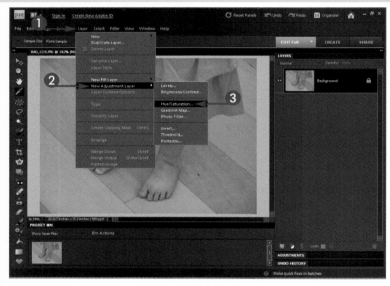

Use the Menu to Add an Adjustment Layer

① Click Layer.

② Select New Adjustment Layer.

③ Select Hue/Saturation.

A New Layer dialog box opens.

④ You can change the layer's name Color by typing it into the Name box or leave it at Hue/Saturation 1.

Leave the other options at the default settings.

⑤ Click OK.

A Hue/Saturation adjustment layer is then created and the Hue/Saturation adjustment panel appears.

1 Click the Adjustment Layer icon ( ) at the bottom of the Layers panel.

2 Select Hue/Saturation.

● The Hue/Saturation adjustment panel opens; it looks nearly identical to the dialog box that you open by selecting Adjust Lighting in the Enhance menu.

● The difference is that an adjustment layer appears automatically over the original picture, now the background layer.

TIPS

Did You Know?
Opening an adjustment layer with the Adjustment Layer icon on the Layers panel is quick and easy. You simply click the black and white circle to get a list of adjustments, and then select the one you want. Opening an adjustment layer with the Layer menu gives you the same list but also includes the ability to name the layer immediately and change its blending mode, its opacity, and how it is grouped with other layers.

Try This!
Naming your layers can help you keep track of what they are doing to your picture. You can name or rename a layer at any time by simply double-clicking the name in the layer and typing a new name.

Did You Know?
The extra menu choices that show up when you click the Adjustment Layer icon in the Layers panel are called *fill layers*. These unique layers enable you to add a color, gradient, or pattern to a layer stack. They are also easily adjustable and do not change the underlying photograph.

Understand
HOW ADJUSTMENT LAYERS WORK

Once you start working with adjustment layers, you will probably use them when beginning your adjustments on the photograph. There will be times when you want to adjust the picture directly, such as when working on a picture you do not need to change. Then you will not use an adjustment layer. But the plusses of using an adjustment layer are so great you will find it worth learning to use them and putting them into your normal workflow.

With adjustment layers, you can always adjust and readjust a picture at maximum quality. This is quite simple to do. You double-click the Adjustment Layer icon with the gears in it. The Adjustments panel immediately reopens and you can make any changes you want. This enables you to tweak an image as you adjust it if you discover you did not make earlier adjustments the way you wanted to.

Apply an Adjustment Layer

① Repeat the steps from the previous page to open the Hue/Saturation dialog box.

② Select Colorize (☐ changes to ☑).

③ Change the Hue and Saturation sliders so the picture looks like it was shot with a strongly colored filter.

④ Click the Eye icon (👁) at the left of the adjustment layer in the Layers panel.

● The new color goes away, yet the adjustment layer is still in the Layers panel.

⑤ Click the Eye icon again (👁).

- The color comes back.

  Clicking the Eye icon (👁) simply turns the visibility of a layer on and off.

47

CONTINUED

⑥ Click the Adjustment Layer icon at (👁) at any time and the Adjustment panel reopens.

⑦ Change the Hue and Saturation sliders to change the color again.

Note: The underlying picture seen as background is not affected, yet the photograph has changed.

 TIPS

Important!

When the Adjustment dialog box of the Adjustments panel is open, everything else in the Photoshop Elements interface is accessible. For example, you can click the Eye icon for a layer and make the layer visibility change if the Hue/Saturation adjustment is open.

Try This!

Using Hue/Saturation to colorize an image can be an interesting way to create a one-color or monochrome photograph. You can change the hue to give the color a bluish cast, a sepia tone, and more. This is a simple way of changing the picture without actually getting rid of the original color picture.

Important!

When you have layers and save your photograph with a PSD or Photoshop file format, all the layers are saved with the file. You can close the image and open it days later — all the layers will still be there. In fact, you can double-click an adjustment layer and go back to exactly what you used before or you can change it.

Chapter 5: Create Adjustment Layers for Nondestructive Changes   111

WORK BLACKS AND WHITES
with a Levels adjustment layer

The workflow that you followed in the first part of this book for adjusting an image is still important: set blacks and whites, adjust midtones, correct color, and so on. Now, however, instead of making these adjustments directly to the picture, you will be making the adjustments with adjustment layers.

Start by adjusting blacks and whites using the Levels adjustment panel. Blacks and whites are critical to how the rest of the picture looks, from its contrast to

its colors, so this is a good place to start your work on an image. Blacks are very subjective. You adjust them differently depending on the subject, your interpretation of that scene, and your experience with working on pictures. Whites are very sensitive and usually have a more limited range of proper adjustment. It is a good idea to name this Levels layer **Blacks-Whites** so you know what it is doing as you add layers later.

① Click Layer.

② Select New Adjustment Layer.

③ Select Levels.

● A New Layer dialog box opens.

④ Change the layer's name to **Blacks-Whites** by typing it in the Name box.

Leave the other options at the default settings.

⑤ Click OK.

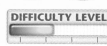

- The Levels adjustment panel opens; it looks nearly identical to the dialog box that you open by selecting Adjust Lighting in the Enhance menu.

6 Adjust blacks by pressing the Alt key as you move the left, black slider.

- A blacks threshold screen appears, showing you where the blacks occur as you adjust.

7 Adjust whites by pressing the Alt key as you move the right, white slider.

- A whites threshold screen appears, showing you where the whites occur as you adjust.

DIFFICULTY LEVEL

TIPS

Did You Know?
Threshold screens show you where certain tones appear in a picture. This is easy to figure out when the tones are either pure black or pure white. The colors show maxed-out channels. Use them when a picture is filled with color and a pure black or white is hard to find.

Get Rid of Layers!
If you decide that the layer you are working on is messed up and you need to get rid of it, it is easy to do. Simply click that layer and drag it up to the Trash Can icon at the bottom right of the Layers panel.

Did You Know?
The histogram, or graph, in the Levels adjustment panel gives you an idea of what needs to be adjusted for blacks and whites. A big gap at either side means that no data is there, which translates as no tones. Most photographs look best when no big gap appears on either side, which is what you aim for when adjusting blacks and whites.

Chapter 5: Create Adjustment Layers for Nondestructive Changes 113

WORK MIDTONES
with a Levels adjustment layer

You first adjust blacks and whites on your photograph with a Levels adjustment layer. Now you will add another Levels adjustment layer to change the midtones. Photoshop Elements does not offer Color Curves as an adjustment layer, so you have to use Levels for midtones. Although Levels does not have as much control over midtones as Color Curves, it offers a lot of flexibility when used as an adjustment layer.

Adjusting midtones is important because it affects the overall brightness or darkness of the picture. Do not use the black slider or white slider for this purpose, even though both seem to affect the overall brightness of the picture.

Name that Levels layer **Midtones** so that you can know exactly which layer is which simply by reading the names. If you follow a consistent workflow, the first layer will always be blacks and whites, and the second layer will be midtones.

1. Click Layer.
2. Select New Adjustment Layer.
3. Select Levels.

• A New Layer dialog box opens.
4. Change the layer's name to **Midtones** by typing it in the Name box.
5. Click OK.

DIFFICULTY LEVEL

- The Levels adjustment panel opens; it looks almost identical to the dialog box that you open by selecting Adjust Lighting in the Enhance menu.

⑥ Adjust the midtones by moving the middle slider left or right.

The photograph and its midtones get brighter as you move the slider to the left.

The photograph and its midtones get darker as you move the slider to the right.

⑦ Click the bar to the right of the Adjustments Panel tab. This collapses the panel.

Click the bar again to reopen the panel.

- Two adjustment layers now sit on top of the original picture and affect how it looks.

TIPS

Try This!
Cropping is important when you are working with layers. You can crop at any time using the technique described in task #17. Cropping occurs across all the layers and is a destructive form of processing, so limit your cropping at first to just getting rid of problems.

Important!
Name your layers. You will find this makes working with layers a lot easier as you add more layers during the process. It can get confusing as to which one is doing what. In addition, named layers can help you see the process used in working on the picture — simply look at the layers from the bottom to the top.

Try This!
The Color Curves adjustment is a good one for midtones, but it is not available as an adjustment layer. Often you will find that your blacks/whites Levels adjustment is pretty standard and can be applied directly to the pixels of your picture. That way you can use the Color Curves adjustment for midtones and use adjustment layers for the rest of your image processing.

CORRECT COLOR
with an adjustment layer

Color casts — subtle colors that creep into an image and contaminate the colors and tones throughout the photograph — can be a problem with any type of photography. Examples include bluish landscapes at sunrise and greenish hair. Color casts were a serious problem when everyone shot film because they could be hard to get rid of. With digital photography, correcting color by removing problem color casts has become a lot easier.

When you correct color with an adjustment layer, you gain a great deal of flexibility. If you decide that a previous color correction is not quite right as you continue to work on a photograph, you can always reopen the adjustment and do it again. This is a great advantage of the nondestructive nature of adjustment layers. In addition, you can use the opacity of the layer to change how strongly the adjustment affects the photograph.

① Click Layer, select New Adjustment Layer, and select Levels.

② Change the layer's name to **Color correction** by typing it in the Name box.

③ Click OK.

④ Click the middle eyedropper in Levels.

⑤ Move the cursor into the picture and click something that should be a neutral white, gray, or black.

This removes a color cast from a neutral tone every time you click.

6 Try clicking different neutral grays throughout the photograph to see what you can get.

Sometimes you can get the right color on the first click, and sometimes it takes a number of clicks.

If you like the overall color, but it is too strong, you can change the Opacity of the layer.

7 Position your cursor over the word *Opacity*.

The cursor changes to a hand with arrows.

8 Click and drag left or right to change the opacity of the layer.

TIPS

Did You Know?
Opacity is the opposite of transparency. Both terms refer to how much you can see through something, a layer in this case. Lower opacity for adjustment layers means the layers' adjustments lose some of their effect.

Important!
The first layers in the workflow described here are all Levels. Although all the adjustments could be made in one Levels control, this would give you a lot less flexibility. By separating the adjustments into separate layers, you can adjust each control individually. This means you can also readjust each control individually.

Did You Know?
As you make more adjustments with Levels, and sometimes with other controls, gaps will begin to appear in the histogram in Levels. These are not necessarily a problem. They become a problem only when tonalities such as gradations in your photograph start to break up. This breakup will be very obvious, looking like steps where there are none, for example.

ENHANCE COLOR
with an adjustment layer

Colors in a photograph often need to be enhanced. The camera simply is not capable of seeing colors in the world the same way you do. Sometimes the camera and sensor capture colors that have an unpleasant color cast in them; correcting it was discussed in the last task. Other times, the colors will be out of sync with what you saw in the scene — colors might be stronger or weaker than what you envisioned for the photograph.

Many times, you need to give a slight boost to the color to make the picture livelier or more dramatic. You can do all these things with a Hue/Saturation adjustment layer. You use this control the same way it was used in task #25.

In this task, you will learn a different way of opening an adjustment layer and renaming it.

1 Click the Adjustment Layer icon ( ) in the Layers panel.

A menu appears.

2 Select Hue/Saturation.

● The Hue/Saturation adjustment appears along with a new adjustment layer.

3 Click and drag the Saturation slider to the right to increase saturation between 5 and 15 points as needed.

④ Click the Master drop-down menu and select a specific color to adjust.

⑤ Move the Saturation slider to the right as needed.

You can increase saturation more when you work with individual colors and still avoid problems.

⑥ Double-click the original Hue/Saturation 1 label for the layer.

⑦ Type a new name, **Enhance colors**.

TIPS

Caution!

When working with Hue/Saturation, be careful that you do not oversaturate colors. This can make the picture look garish and unattractive very quickly. It is tempting to increase the saturation of your picture to make the colors look bright and lively, but this can also create a harsh quality for the image.

More Options!

You can readjust the panel bin to make it display the layers in your Layers panel better. For example, the Undo History panel does not need as much space as the Layers panel often does. You can click and drag the dividing line between these panels to make them smaller or larger.

Did You Know?

You can change the size of the layers in the Layers panel. You may want them bigger so that the icon appears larger. Do this by clicking the menu icon at the top of the panel, and then going to the bottom of that drop-down menu and selecting Panel Options. This gives you choices for the size of layers.

FIX PROBLEM EXPOSURES
with layer blending modes

At times your picture may be simply too dark or too light. There are many reasons why this can happen. Sometimes the camera makes a mistake in exposure, or sometimes the photographer sets the camera wrong. Regardless, you end up with a picture that needs immediate correction, either to make it brighter or make it darker.

Photoshop Elements gives you an interesting way to do this in its layer blending modes. You need to add an adjustment layer to your photograph. It really

does not matter which adjustment you choose because you will not be using the adjustment layer for its original adjustment purpose. You are simply using this layer so that Photoshop Elements has something to work with when communicating between layers, which is what layer blending modes do. When you first open the blending modes, you see a long list of choices — ignore them and concentrate on two key modes for photographers: Multiply and Screen.

Fix a Too-Bright Photograph

① Click the Adjustment Layer icon (▨) and select Levels.

● The new adjustment layer appears in the Layers panel.

② Click the blending modes drop-down menu, which says Normal by default.

③ Click Multiply.

● The whole photo darkens by about one f-stop.

Fix a Too-Dark Photograph

① Click the Adjustment Layer icon and select Levels.

● The new adjustment layer appears in the Layers panel.

② Click the Blending Modes drop-down menu, which says Normal by default.

③ Click Screen.

● The whole photo lightens by about one f-stop.

 TIPS

Caution!

These blending modes are no substitute for good exposure. They really can help when you run into problems and challenges with specific images, but you should not use them as a habit because they can only fix limitations in the picture and not capture what was originally in the scene.

More Options!

Noise can be a problem when you use Screen as a blending mode. Noise is always in a picture but is usually well hidden in the darkest parts of the image. Because Screen brightens those dark areas, it also often reveals noise. That is not a problem of Screen, but a fact of life for digital photography.

Did You Know?

Neither Screen nor Multiply have controls other than on or off. You either use them or you do not. However, the layers that they affect do have an important control that you can use, Opacity. With Opacity, you can reduce the effect of Screen or Multiply as you reduce the opacity.

Understand
HOW LAYER MASKS WORK

Layer masks are an important part of Photoshop Elements and well worth learning even though they are not very intuitive. They change how an adjustment layer works in a nondestructive way. Very often a photograph needs to be adjusted in different ways across the image. It may be too bright in one area or the wrong color in another. Chapter 4 describes how to use selections to control adjustments in specific areas. Layer masks increase this type of control, and unlike selections, they can always be changed. Layer masks can also be combined with selections to get even more control.

Layer masks either allow the adjustment of an adjustment layer to work or they block it. White in a layer mask allows the adjustment, whereas black blocks it. By applying white or black to a layer mask, you can then effectively control specific areas in a photograph and, in those areas, whether an adjustment works (white) or is not allowed to work (black).

Note: Use the dark photo you lightened in the previous task as it has only one adjustment layer.

● The white box in the adjustment layer is an icon for the layer mask.

❶ Click the Paintbrush in the toolbox.

❷ Right-click the picture to get the brush size menu and choose a moderate-size brush.

❸ Click the small white-over-black icon below the colors at the bottom of the toolbox.

This resets your foreground, or top, and background, or bottom, colors.

❹ Click the curved arrow between the foreground and background so that black is on top.

The top color is the foreground color and the color for your brush.

5 Click and paint two lines across your picture to create an X.

● A dark X now appears in the layer mask icon.

You did not draw a dark X on the picture, but in the layer mask.

The black X in the layer mask then blocks the original adjustment, which creates the effect in the picture.

DIFFICULTY LEVEL

6 Click the curved arrow between the foreground and background colors so that white is on top.

7 Paint out the X in your photograph by painting white over the black.

● This removes the black, which then allows the effect of the adjustment layer to reappear.

TIPS

Important!

Throughout this book, you have seen the toolbox in its default, one-column display. This does not show the foreground-background colors because of the screen resolution used for the book. So in this and further tasks, you will see the toolbox displayed as two columns. You can change your display from one to two columns by clicking the double-arrow at the top of the toolbox.

Important!

Layer masks affect what a layer does but not the actual adjustment. This is an important distinction. Putting black in a layer mask might block a darkening effect and make the picture brighter, or it could block a brightening effect and make the picture darker. You have to think in terms of black blocking an effect and not creating its own effect.

Practice!

Layer masks can be counterintuitive for the photographer. Yet they are an extremely important tool to understand. You can do it! It just takes practice. You have to add adjustment layers with different sorts of controls and then paint in black and white to see how the layer mask works to block or allow those adjustments.

REMOVE ADJUSTMENTS
with black

Once you start working with layer masks, you will learn the real power of adjustment layers. It is very common to do early adjustments such as setting blacks and whites in a picture and run into a problem with the range of tones. For example, when adjusting most of the whites in the picture properly, you may find one small area gets overadjusted. If you try to adjust Levels for that one white, the rest of the picture does not get the proper adjustment.

Fortunately, you have a layer mask associated with every adjustment layer. You can make the correct adjustment for the overall picture and ignore what happens with one small part such as that small area of white. You simply use a black brush and paint over that problem part of the picture. That blocks the adjustment and gives you much more control over your picture.

① Open a photo that has a contrast challenge with something very bright.

● In this photo, adjusting the whites for the chaparral plants on the hills makes the clouds wash out.

② Click the Paintbrush in the toolbox.

③ If black is not the foreground color, click the curved arrow between the foreground and background colors so that black is on top.

④ Click on Size in the brush options bar and size your brush appropriate to the problem.

⑤ Paint black over the problem to block the adjustment.

● The layer mask icon indicates the painted area.

 # 54

⑥ Change your brush size as needed to block or allow the adjustment in other areas.

TIPS

More Options!

You can change how strong the blocking effect of black is, or the effect of white, by changing the Opacity of the brush. You make the adjustment in the options bar above the photograph. A number of options are here for affecting how a brush works.

Remember This!

As you gain experience working on layer masks, you will discover that you are constantly changing the brush size to match the needs of your photograph. Remember that this is easy to do by using the bracket keys to the right of the letter P — the opening bracket ([ ) makes the brush smaller and the closing bracket ( ]) makes it larger.

Important!

Once you start working with more than one adjustment layer, you have to be sure you are in the right layer and layer mask. It can be frustrating and confusing if you start painting in the wrong layer mask. To be sure, you can simply click the layer mask icon in the correct layer in the Layers panel. The correct layer is also highlighted in black.

Chapter 5: Create Adjustment Layers for Nondestructive Changes

ADD ADJUSTMENTS
using black and then white

Sometimes you will run into a photograph that simply needs an adjustment in one area but not in the rest of the image. You could try adjusting the whole picture and then blocking out everything in it, doing a lot of work with a black paintbrush. If there really is only a small area that needs to be adjusted, that can be a lot of work.

There is a better way. You first make the adjustment as best you can for the small area that needs the

change. You ignore what happens in the rest of the photograph. Then you block the entire adjustment by filling the entire layer mask with black. Next you take a white paintbrush and bring the adjustment back in only in the areas where you want it. Essentially you are adding an adjustment to a very specific area without affecting the entire picture.

Identify the Problem

① Open and adjust a photo that has a small area that needs adjustment compared to the rest of the picture.

● In this photo, the overall image of highbush blueberry flowers looks fine, but the bumblebee is too dark.

② Add an adjustment that will correct the problem area even though it makes the whole picture look wrong.

● A Levels adjustment layer was added to this photo without adjustment.

● Then the Screen mode was selected.

● The bee looks much better now, but the rest of the picture is too bright.

Add Black

1 Click Edit.

2 Select Fill Layer.

DIFFICULTY LEVEL

● The Fill Layer dialog box appears.

3 Click the Use drop-down menu and select Black.

Leave the other options at their defaults.

4 Click OK.

TIPS

More Options!

Often you need to switch back and forth between black and white as you work on the layer mask. This makes it easy to block or unblock an effect from an adjustment layer. You can quickly and easily change your brush color by pressing the X key to switch between black and white.

More Options!

You may be working on a picture and find that the layer mask gets confusing. You cannot tell what you have or have not done. To start with a clean slate, you can fill the layer mask with white by using the Fill Layer under the Edit menu but choosing white instead of black.

Try This!

When working with the Multiply or Screen blending modes, you may find that the first use of the mode helps but is not enough. If you duplicate this layer, you can increase the effect even more. Duplicate the layer by dragging it to the New Layer icon (⬛), which is to the left of the Adjustment Layer icon (⬛).

ADD ADJUSTMENTS
using black and then white

A common problem in photographs is a lack of balance among the tones. The camera wants to interpret the scene very differently than your eyes do. You can see all the detail from bright to dark areas just fine, but the camera cannot. To bring that picture back to balance, you need to make some adjustments in Photoshop Elements.

This is where layer masks really shine. You can very carefully choose exactly what areas of the picture are going to be affected by any individual adjustment. That can either mean blocking an overadjustment or allowing a small area of a very specific adjustment, as shown in this example. You will sometimes hear people say that this is "cheating." That comes from a lack of understanding of how photography really works. You should be able to control your picture to interpret it closer to what you really saw.

● The photo now has a Screen adjustment layer, but its effect is blocked by the black in the layer mask.

The picture looks as if no Screen adjustment has been made at all.

Adjust the Whites

❶ Select the Paintbrush tool.

❷ Change the foreground color to white.

❸ Change your brush size to match the area that needs to be adjusted.

④ Paint the brush with the white foreground color over the area that needs to be changed.

The adjustment is now allowed, but only in that area.

⑤ Change the foreground color to black.

⑥ Make a smaller brush.

⑦ Paint over problems along the edge between adjusted and unadjusted areas.

The black brush now blocks the adjustment again to fix the edge.

TIPS

Important!
Generally you will want to use soft-edged brushes for the layer mask. Soft brushes enable you to better blend the adjusted and the unadjusted areas. Hard-edged brushes can cause problems by making your brush lines show up. Use them sparingly.

More Options!
Selections can be used in a layer mask. This can be important if you want to adjust something up to a very tight edge. It is better to make a selection and paint black or white right up along the edge of the selection instead of trying to use a hard-edged brush. This gives you a better edge. See task #56 for more about selections.

Important!
Edges are very important. One thing that often gives away a poorly adjusted image is the edge between an adjusted and unadjusted area. Pay close attention to what is happening along that edge. Use smaller brushes for a tight edge or larger brushes for a soft edge. And when you have a very tight edge, use a selection, even changing the feathering.

COMBINE LAYER MASKS
with selections

Everything you learned about selections still applies when working with adjustment layers and layer masks. Sometimes it is easier to simply paint an effect on or off the picture by using white or black, but other times your workflow is more efficient if you create a selection first. When you create a selection and then add an adjustment layer, a layer mask is automatically created for you based on that selection.

A selection limits an effect to one area and blocks the effect outside that area. A layer mask limits an effect to an area controlled by white and blocks the effect where the mask is black. Making a selection, and then adding an adjustment layer creates a layer mask with white as the selected area and black outside the selection. Selections can be very helpful when very specific areas need to be adjusted, such as creating dark edges for a photograph.

① Make a selection around the subject, inside the outer edges.

② Invert the selection by clicking Select and then Inverse.

③ Open a Brightness/Contrast adjustment layer from the Adjustment Layer icon in the Layers panel.

④ Reduce Brightness to about −25 to −30.

● The layer mask is controlling the effect, but the edge is very sharp and unattractive.

130

5 Click Filter.

6 Select Blur.

7 Select Gaussian Blur.

56

DIFFICULTY LEVEL

The Gaussian Blur dialog box opens.

8 Click and drag the Radius slider to a high amount.

Depending on the photograph, this can be as low as 40 or as high as more than 200.

9 Click OK.

A soft darkness is applied to the outer edges of the photo.

TIPS

Did You Know?
Using Gaussian Blur for blending edges has a lot of advantages over using feathering with selections. Feathering must be done to a specific number, and then you click OK and look to see if the effect is what you want. With Gaussian Blur and a layer mask, you can change the Radius and watch the blending occur in real time.

More Options!
When you first open Gaussian Blur, the edge might not appear blurred in the preview box. Simply move your cursor into the picture and click the edge. That immediately places the black-white edge inside the preview box so you can see what happens as Gaussian Blur is increased.

Important!
A great advantage of adjustment layers is the ability to change the adjustment. In this edge-darkening technique, for example, you can always click the icon for the Brightness/Contrast adjustment layer and reopen the Adjustment panel. You can then change that edge darkness as desired.

BALANCE COLORS AND TONES
in a picture

A common challenge photographers face is a picture that is not balanced visually to match the composition or the way that people really see a subject. If you look at a scene, for example, your eye balances out the brightness levels so that you can easily see and compare elements of that scene. The camera does no such thing. If the left side of a scene is brighter than the right, the camera shows it just that way, creating an imbalance in the tones of the picture compared to the way you see the scene. Colors can have a similar problem when one color starts to dominate the picture because it is too saturated compared to the others.

Through the use of adjustment layers and layer masks, you can fix this imbalance and help your photographs communicate something much closer to what you originally saw when you took the picture.

❶ Click the Adjustment Layer icon to open a Levels adjustment layer to correct an imbalance in brightness.

❷ Adjust the sliders until the problem area looks better, such as the sky in this photo.

● Ignore what happens in the rest of the photo because it will be overadjusted.

57

③ Click the Gradient tool in the toolbox.

④ Click the curved arrow between the foreground and background colors so that white is on top.

⑤ Click your cursor first in the area where you want to keep your adjustment.

⑥ Drag your cursor into the area where you want to remove the adjustment.

● The Gradient tool puts white in the first area, black in the second area, and creates a blend between them.

The image now has its tonalities better blended.

TIPS

Did You Know?

If you get the white and black parts of the Gradient tool mixed up, do not worry. That is actually a common challenge when first learning to use the Gradient tool. If you click and drag and the black and white show up in the wrong places, simply do it again in the reverse direction.

More Options!

You may need to do multiple applications of the Gradient tool before the picture looks right. Sometimes the angle will be wrong, other times the gradient will be too short and too obvious, and other times the gradient will be too long and ineffective. Keep trying until your picture looks right.

Important!

Change the adjustment as needed after you use the Gradient tool. Sometimes you will guess wrong as to the correct amount of adjustment to properly balance the picture. When you apply the Gradient tool, the picture may look too dark or too light. Simply reopen that adjustment layer and readjust as needed.

BRING OUT SHADOW DETAIL
in specific areas

As you look to balance a picture's tonalities, you often discover small areas that are too dark. These are typically shadows that did not get the same light as the rest of the picture. Yet for the picture to really look right, for it to be interpreted closer to the way you saw a scene, these dark areas need to be increased in brightness.

Once again the adjustment layer and its layer mask come to the rescue. You use a blending mode again,

the Screen mode to brighten the dark area, and then the layer mask to limit that change just to the area needed. Although this works very well, one thing you may notice occurring is an increase in noise in those dark areas. There is nothing you can do about that. Revealing detail in dark areas often means revealing the noise that is there as well.

① Open a Levels adjustment layer by clicking the Adjustment Layer icon in the Layers panel.

② Make no adjustments.

③ Click the Blending Modes drop-down menu, which says Normal by default.

④ Select Screen.

The lightening effect of Screen is applied to the whole picture.

5 Open the Fill Layer dialog box from the Edit menu.

6 Select Black in the Use drop-down menu in the Contents area.

7 Click OK.

DIFFICULTY LEVEL

The lightening effect of Screen is blocked.

8 Click the Paintbrush in the toolbox.

9 Choose a brush size appropriate to the area being adjusted.

10 Choose white for the foreground color.

11 Paint in the lightening effect.

 TIPS

Important!

Edges are critical when you are dealing with small areas of change in a photograph and using a layer mask. A sloppily painted edge is very obvious in the picture and distracts the viewer even to the point of the truth of your picture coming into question.

Apply It!

Work your edges by going back and forth between white and black brushes. In addition, change the size of your brushes by using the bracket keys as you go. If you are really having trouble with an edge, try using a selection to control where the black and white go within your layer mask.

More Options!

You can actually see your layer mask in black and white over your photograph. Position your cursor over the layer mask icon in the layer you are working on. Press the Alt/Opt key as you click the Layer Mask icon and the layer mask will appear where your picture is. Press Alt/Opt and click again to get back to your picture.

DARKEN HIGHLIGHT DETAIL
in specific areas

As you continue to balance a picture's tonalities, you often find too-bright areas. These are typically highlight areas that received more light than your subject. When you expose properly for the subject, your photograph will look good where the subject is but these highlight areas will look overexposed. Once again, for the picture to look right, such out-of-balance bright areas need to be balanced, this time brought down in tone.

You use the adjustment layer and its layer mask again, but this time using the Multiply blending mode to darken the right area. The layer mask is used to limit that change just to the area needed. Luckily, no noise problems can come from darkening a bright area, but there are limits as to how much darkening you can do if the area is too overexposed.

① Open a Levels adjustment layer by clicking the Adjustment Layer icon in the Layers panel.

② Make no adjustments.

③ Click the Blending Modes drop-down menu, which says Normal by default.

④ Select Multiply.

- The darkening effect of Multiply is applied to the whole picture.

5 Open the Fill Layer dialog box from the Edit menu.

6 Select Black in the Use drop-down menu in Contents.

7 Click OK.

The darkening effect of Multiply is blocked.

8 Click the Paintbrush in the toolbox.

9 Choose a brush size appropriate to the area being adjusted.

10 Choose white for the foreground color.

11 Paint in the darkening effect.

- The Levels Layer Mask icon indicates the painted area.

TIPS

Important!

Exposure is very important when dealing with bright and highlighted areas in a photograph. If a bright area is too washed out, no amount of work in Photoshop Elements will bring in any detail. When bright areas in a picture absolutely have to have detail, they must be captured when you take the picture.

Did You Know?

Sometimes when you make a correction to a specific area in the photograph, the whole photograph changes in its appearance, maybe looking too bright or too dark overall. You can simply go back to your midtones adjustment layer, reopen the adjustment, and make a correction.

More Options!

You do not have to limit your adjustments to simply fixing a bright area or a dark area. If your photograph needs help in both areas, then use two different adjustment layers, one set to Multiply and one set to Screen, and then use the layer masks appropriately to fix both places.

Add a
GRADUATED FILTER EFFECT

Skies can be a bold and beautiful part of an outdoor photograph, yet skies are often much different in brightness compared to the ground. Skies often look a lot better in real life than they do in a photograph, which is generally due to the out-of-balance way the camera sees the world compared to the way people do. When the sky is brought into balance with the rest of the picture, photographs often come alive and

much better express the feelings the photographer had when she originally took the picture.

Many photographers use a filter called a *graduated neutral density filter* that enables them to darken the sky without darkening the ground. If you have good detail in the sky, you can mimic this effect in Photoshop Elements to get a more dramatic sky and a better interpretation of your scene.

① Open a Levels adjustment layer by clicking the Adjustment Layer icon in the Layers panel.

② Make no adjustments.

③ Click the Blending Modes drop-down menu, which says Normal by default.

④ Select Multiply.

- The darkening effect of Multiply is applied to the whole picture.

5 Click the Gradient tool in the toolbox.

6 Choose white for the foreground color.

7 Click your cursor in the middle part of the sky.

8 Drag your cursor down to the ground.

60

DIFFICULTY LEVEL

- The effect of the Multiply layer is now applied only to the sky at its maximum effect.

9 Lower the Opacity setting if the sky is too dark.

- The Levels Layer Mask icon indicates the painted area.

- The effect blends very naturally with the use of the Gradient tool down to the ground.

TIPS

Important!

The key to this technique for creating a graduated filter effect is in the blend, the distance of the gradient. If the picture does not look right, especially if there is too hard an edge between the dark and the light areas, reapply your gradient with a bigger distance between the starting and ending points.

Try This!

After you apply your gradient and make the sky look good, you may discover there are some areas in the ground that look too bright. Simply take a white brush and brush over those areas so the darkening effect of the Multiply mode can appear on those areas as well.

Try This!

One challenge with this technique is that the gradient can cover tall objects that extend into the sky from the ground. You could never correct this with a graduated filter over a lens. You can correct it in Photoshop Elements by using a black paintbrush to paint over these objects and block the darkening effect.

FLATTEN LAYERS
when done

After working on your photo, you will come to the point where you are more or less done with it. You can save and store this photo as is, using a Photoshop PSD file, and keep all its layers. Sometimes, however, you may want a simpler file that you can quickly use for purposes other than adjusting a picture. The PSD file format is not generally recognized outside of Adobe programs.

At this point, it is a good idea to flatten the image, merging the layers together into a simplified image file, and then save the picture in the appropriate format. If you are going to use a photo for the Web or e-mail, choose a JPEG file. If you are preparing pictures for use in a brochure or other publication, you might decide to use a TIFF file. You can flatten an image using the Layer menu or through the Layers panel drop-down menu.

Use the Menu to Flatten

① Click Layer.

② Select Flatten Image.

Use the Panel Menu to Flatten

① Click the panel menu icon at the right of the Layers tab.

This icon is a set of horizontal lines and can be hard to see.

A drop-down menu appears.

② Select Flatten Image.

● All layers and their effects are now merged.

Save the Flattened Image

❶ Click File.

❷ Select Save As.

The Save As dialog box appears.

Choose the appropriate file format, change the file name and folder location if needed, and then click OK.

TIPS

Did You Know?

Some photographers save all their layered files forever, just in case they want to revise the pictures. Other photographers find that saving all these layered files can get to be unwieldy and unnecessary for their workflow. There is no arbitrary right or wrong to this. It depends entirely on how comfortable you are with your work.

Important!

Once your file is flattened and closed, you have no access to the original layers. If you flatten the file, you can always undo this in the Undo History panel if the picture is still open. But if an image is flattened and closed, that opportunity is gone and the layers are gone as well.

Try This!

You can combine all your layers and their effects into a single layer on top of the layer stack so that you have access to a "flattened file" and layers at the same time. Click the top layer and then press Ctrl+Shift+Alt+E or Cmd+Shift+Opt+E. This merges the layers and then creates a new layer with that image on top of the layer stack.

Solve Photo Problems

You always want to take the best possible picture when you squeeze the shutter on your camera. You do not want to have to fix problems in the picture that could be correct if the picture were taken more carefully from the start. Yet, no matter how hard you work, sooner or later you are going to have some problems in a photograph to fix.

These can be all sorts of things, such as dust on the sensor, unwanted light flare, blank skies, and more. They are not anyone's fault, but can crop up in a picture due to many factors, and keep that picture from being all that it can be. Sometimes these problems are

extremely annoying and very distracting to a viewer. Other times, they particularly frustrate the photographer. Regardless, you want them out of your picture.

Photoshop Elements includes some excellent tools to deal with problems in the picture after you have done your basic processing. Some of them do take some time and practice to master, however. Do not be discouraged if you try something like the Clone tool and your results are not perfect at first. With practice and experience, you can master any tool in Photoshop Elements.

Top 100

CLONE OUT
problems

Cloning works essentially by copying a small part of the photograph from one area and then pasting that copy onto a new location in the photograph. This occurs without you having to copy or paste. All you have to do is select a spot to copy from and a place to copy over. You tell Photoshop Elements where you want the cloning to start from, how big of a copy you want to make, and where to place the copy.

You set a "clone-from" point by pressing Alt or Option as you click over the good part of the photo. You tell Photoshop Elements how big a copy you want to make by the size you choose for your brush. Finally, you click multiple times over your problem area and the program knows where to place the little copy under the cloning point.

There are two problems in this photo: the stray rock on the left and the unwanted chair leg at the top right.

1. Click the Zoom tool, or magnifier, at the top of the toolbox.

2. Click and drag your cursor around the problem area to magnify it.

3. Click the New Layer icon in the Layers palette.

● This creates a new, empty layer.

4. Name the layer **Clone Layer**.

5 Click the Clone Stamp tool in the toolbox.

6 Right-click the photograph to open the brush menu to quickly select a specific size of brush.

7 Pick a brush size appropriate to the problem.

● Leave Mode at Normal, Opacity 100%, and Aligned selected.

8 Select Sample All Layers (☐ changes to ☑).

62

9 Press Alt/Opt as you click an area near your problem that is problem free.

This sets the clone-from point.

Did You Know?
For most cloning, you will use the Aligned option for the Clone Stamp tool. This keeps the clone-from point aligned at the same distance and angle to your clone-to point as you clone. If your clone-from area is very small, deselect Aligned so that the clone-from point always goes back to that area.

Try This!
If you run into trouble with the settings of any tool, including the Clone Stamp tool, you can quickly reset the tool back to its defaults. Click the small down arrow at the far left of the options toolbar over the toolbox. This gives you a menu with the reset option. Usually you can just select Reset Tool.

Try This!
Once you magnify the area where you are cloning, you may need to adjust the position of that area slightly. If you press the spacebar, the cursor changes to a Hand icon. Keep pressing the spacebar and then click and drag the picture to move it around. This works with any tool in Photoshop Elements.

CLONE OUT
problems

A common problem comes from objects appearing around the subject that you did not see when you took the photograph. This can occur when you concentrate so hard on the subject that you do not see the rest of the photo. Such inadvertent objects can be very annoying and distracting. Other problems can include undesirable *lens flare* — the little light spots and circles near a bright light — or a misplaced piece of trash in the picture.

The Clone Stamp tool is a very powerful way of covering up such problems. You can clone to a blank layer, click as you go for each clone spot rather than brushing continuously, reset your clone-from point whenever you see problems, and change your brush size as you go. By doing these things, your cloning will look more natural, without repeating patterns called *cloning artifacts*.

⑩ Click over the problem area.

Click multiple times to cover the problem.

Change your clone-from point to keep the clone work blending.

⑪ Continue clicking the problem areas.

Because you are on a layer, there is no problem if your cloning goes too far.

⑫ If it does, click the Eraser tool.

⑬ Right-click the image to get the brush menu and choose a small brush size.

⑭ Erase the problem from the layer.

There is no effect on the rest of the photo.

 # 62 CONTINUED

15 When cloning over areas with distinct lines, center your clone-from point over a line by pressing Alt/Opt, and then click when the crosshairs are lined up with the line.

16 Center your clone-to point over the continuation of that line into the problem area by pressing Alt/Opt to get the crosshairs, but then release Alt/Opt before clicking.

17 Click and clone over the problem.

The lines should line up.

If they do not line up, undo the work and reset the clone-from and clone-to points.

TIPS

Try This!

If cloning starts to look messy, take the Eraser tool and erase the work. Because you are working to a layer, you are only erasing something applied over the actual picture. You can always turn the visibility of the layer on and off to see this by clicking the Eye icon () at the left side of the layer.

Important!

To do cloning well takes practice. At first, it takes some time as you continually change your clone-from point and brush size so that the cloning blends well. It is important to do this because poorly done cloning draws attention to itself very quickly.

Did You Know?

Dust spots in the sky from sensor dust can be cleaned up using the Spot Healing Brush ( ). This tool is in the group of tools just above the Eraser. With it, you simply click the dust spot and Photoshop Elements copies something nearby over that spot and helps it blend. You can also use this tool with layers — select Sample All Layers in the options bar.

REMOVE PEOPLE FROM A SCENE
with Photomerge Scene Cleaner

There are so many wonderful photo opportunities in public areas. These places attract a lot of people as well. This often means that photographing in some areas without people getting into your shot can be difficult.

Sometimes you can wait until a gap occurs in the flow of the crowd so that you get a picture without people. But often you cannot, especially if you are traveling with family who want to move on and see the other sights of the area.

Photoshop Elements's Photomerge Scene Cleaner enables you to remove people from a scene. You have to shoot multiple pictures of that scene so that the people walking through it are not all in one place. Shoot from the same position, with the same exposure and hold your camera as steady as possible so that the overall framing of your picture does not change much. You can adjust individual shots to match exposure if needed.

① Open the series of photos you need to clean up in the Project Bin.

They should all appear in the Project Bin.

② Select the whole group by clicking the first photo, then press Shift as you click the last photo.

③ Click File.

④ Select New.

⑤ Select Photomerge Scene Cleaner.

The Photomerge Scene Cleaner opens.

- A how-to panel also appears.

⑥ Drag the best photo of your group into the Final photo window.

⑦ Drag a different picture into the Source window.

⑧ Click the Pencil Tool in the how-to panel.

⑨ Draw around the object you want to remove in the Final frame.

⑩ Alternately, draw around an area in the Source window that you want to move to the Final frame.

Photomerge moves parts of the Source photo appropriately to the Final photo.

Note: What you see here is the result of step 9; you do not see step 10. When you are done circling areas, the program updates and shows you where the area came from that is doing the scene cleanup.

⑪ Click Done when you are finished.

The photo opens as a new image into Edit Full with layers holding the work you did.

TIPS

Did You Know?

Photoshop Elements includes some pretty amazing alignment work in its Photomerge feature. In order to match everything in the Scene Cleaner, the picture elements within the scene must line up. The program analyzes the pictures and lines them up for you. It helps to keep the image frame lined up as best you can while you shoot.

Try This!

The Scene Cleaner may not work immediately the way you want it to. Undo your work, and then try drawing around a different part of the picture, drawing tighter to an area, and drawing in both the Source and the Final images because you will get different results.

Try This!

Once you are done using the Scene Cleaner, you may discover that the photograph still has some imperfections. Instead of trying to do it all over again in the Scene Cleaner, it may be quicker and easier to use the Clone Stamp tool to make small corrections as needed.

Fix problems due to
LENS DISTORTION

Many photographers have discovered the benefits of large-range zooms that go from very wide angles to extreme telephoto focal lengths, such as 18-200mm or 28-300mm. These lenses offer a lot of focal-length options in one lens, making them ideal for travel as well as a convenient way of always being prepared for whatever your subject might be. These lenses are available for digital single lens reflex (dSLR) cameras, and come built into many advanced compact digital cameras.

Such extreme focal length changes in one lens, however, challenge lens manufacturers. Most of these lenses have something called *barrel distortion*, especially common when shot at wider focal lengths. This causes a curving outward of straight lines near the top, bottom, or sides of the photograph. You can correct this in Photoshop Elements in the Correct Camera Distortion filter, even though you are actually correcting lens distortion. You can only apply this to actual pixels of a photo, so this will not work if you are working on an adjustment layer.

① Click Filter.

② Select Correct Camera Distortion.

The Correct Camera Distortion window opens.

③ Click the Remove Distortion slider and move it left or right to correct a curved horizon.

④ Use the grid to help you determine when the line is straight.

5 Correct any crooked horizons by clicking the Angle icon and dragging the pointer.

6 You can also correct crooked photos by typing a number in the angle degrees box.

7 Adjust the Edge Extension slider until the edges are solid, with no gaps.

8 When you have corrected the photo, click OK.

The photo opens into Edit Full with your work displayed as a single layer.

 TIPS

More Options!

You can wait to fix the frame edges until the photo is back in the main Photoshop Elements work area. Sometimes this gives you more options for the final look of the image. In this case, do not use the Edge Extension slider. Instead, use the Crop tool in Photoshop Elements to crop out the distorted edges of the final photo.

Try This!

After you have used your camera and its lens or lenses, you will learn what focal lengths create the most distortion. You can then try to avoid the problem when shooting by keeping strong horizontal or vertical lines away from the edges of the photograph. You can also disguise those edges by having something in the photo cut across them, such as a tree or a rock.

Try This!

The Vignette controls in the Correct Camera Distortion window are designed to correct uneven brightness from the center to the corners of the picture. Some lenses, especially wide-angle focal lengths of long-range zooms, darken the outside parts of the picture; you can correct such images using the Vignette sliders.

FIX PERSPECTIVE PROBLEMS
with building photographs

Buildings stand tall, but when you photograph them, they often look like they are falling over backward. This is because when you get close to a building and point your camera up to photograph it, the camera and lens accentuate perspective so that the building appears smaller at the top than at the bottom. This is especially common with wide-angle focal lengths. In the past, you had to use very expensive gear to correct it, which meant architectural photography was

not as accessible for the average photographer. In many situations, a leaning building weakens the look of the building.

Correct Camera Distortion once again comes to the rescue. Although the filter is commonly used for buildings, you can also use it for tall trees, cliffs, and other tall objects. By straightening up these objects, they gain a very majestic look in your photograph.

① Click Filter.

② Select Correct Camera Distortion.

The Correct Camera Distortion window opens.

③ Click the Vertical Perspective slider and move it to the left to vertically straighten a building.

④ Use the grid to help you determine when the building is straight.

#65

DIFFICULTY LEVEL

⑤ Click the Horizontal Perspective slider and move it to the left or right to correct the horizontal perspective.

⑥ Correct any left or right lean with the Angle icon.

Note: The Angle icon is very sensitive, so you may find it easier to type numbers in the angle degree box.

⑦ Use the Edge Extension slider, if possible, to bring back important parts of the picture.

⑧ When you have corrected the photo, click OK.

● The photo opens into Edit Full with your work displayed as a single layer.

⑨ Click the Crop tool in the toolbox.

⑩ Use the Crop tool to crop out the distorted edges of the final picture.

⑪ Click the green check mark icon when you are finished.

TIPS

Did You Know?

In order to control perspective in the past, such as leaning buildings, photographers had to use special equipment. They would use perspective control lenses that allowed them to move the lens to get a whole building into the scene instead of tilting the camera. A view camera offered the same control.

Try This!

As you adjust the perspective of your picture, you may find you lose certain parts of the image. Often there is nothing you can do about that. In that case, use your Crop tool creatively. Instead of trying to get everything into the picture, which cannot be done, crop your picture so that it looks interesting.

Try This!

When you tilt the camera up at a tall building, perspective always makes it look as though it is falling backward. If you use a very wide-angle lens and get very close to the building, this can be a dramatic effect and not something you want to correct.

Chapter 6: Solve Photo Problems 153

REMOVE DEAD SPACE
with Recompose

Sometimes people and objects do not cooperate when you photograph them. When you get extra space around your subject, you can use the Crop tool to remove pixels that do not belong in the picture. But what if those extra spaces are in between subjects, such as a mom and daughter standing too far apart, a soccer game where players and ball are separated too much compared to the reality of the game, and so forth?

A new tool in Photoshop Elements 8 called the Recompose tool enables you to deal with such problems. When you are using this tool, Photoshop Elements very smartly examines your picture to find important objects in it. Then as you change the size of the picture, Photoshop Elements keeps the important objects at the same size while carving out dead space in between them. The results can be quite remarkable.

1 Click and hold the Crop tool.

New choices appear.

2 Select Recompose Tool.

● The Adobe Photoshop Elements how-to window opens with instructions on using the tool.

3 If you do not need this window, select Don't show again (☐ changes to ☑).

4 Click OK.

#66

DIFFICULTY LEVEL

5 Click a control box along the edge of the photograph.

When your cursor changes to a double arrow, you are over the box.

6 Drag the side in to have Photoshop Elements smartly crop and recompose the photo.

7 Click the green check mark icon when you are done.

Photoshop Elements processes the recomposition to make this change work.

The image appears as a layer.

8 Click and hold the Recompose tool to select the Crop tool from the toolbox.

9 Use the Crop tool to crop out the blank edges of the final picture.

10 Click the green check mark icon when you are finished.

TIPS

Caution!

Be careful of altering reality. Bringing a soccer ball closer to the players in this example is accurate for the conditions. The timing of the shot captured the ball farther away from the players than it had actually been. But you can change the image so much that the photograph becomes a lie. If you simply tighten up a photo where people were captured too far apart, it is altering a photo, but not reality if these people were originally closer together. Change as much as you want if you are after a fantasy image; it will label it as such.

Try This!

For more precise control, use the green and red brushes. You will find them at the top of the photo in the options bar for the Recompose tool. Choose the green brush, and then paint over areas you want to protect so Photoshop Elements will protect them as you change the size of the photo. Choose the red brush and paint over areas you want to remove.

Make an
OUT-OF-FOCUS BACKGROUND

A good background in a photo can really set your subject. But for a variety of reasons, sometimes you simply cannot take a picture of your subject in front of a great background. This can be especially true if you are taking a snapshot of family with a little point-and-shoot camera you just happened to have in your pocket.

One way of improving backgrounds is to make them out of focus. Sometimes you can do this when you are taking the picture, but you can also blur the background behind your subject in Photoshop Elements. The latter action can give you more control over your background, although it can be a challenge to make it look right. Although you can use selections to blur a background, you will find you get faster results and they look better when you use layers.

① Click your flattened photo.

② Press Ctrl/Cmd+J twice to duplicate your layer twice.

● Duplicate layers appear over your original.

③ Click the top layer's Eye icon to turn it off.

④ Click the middle layer to select it.

⑤ Click Filter.

⑥ Select Blur.

⑦ Select Gaussian Blur.

- The Gaussian Blur dialog box appears.

⑧ Click and drag the Radius slider until the background looks out of focus.

⑨ Ignore what is happening to the subject.

⑩ Click OK.

⑪ Click the top layer's Eye icon to turn the layer back on.

⑫ Click the top layer to select it.

⑬ Click the Eraser tool in the toolbox.

⑭ Select a good size for the Eraser based on the area of the background, and change the size as you go.

⑮ Click and drag to erase the sharp parts of the top photo layer so the underlying blurred parts show through.

If you go too far, use the Undo History palette or press Ctrl/Cmd+Z to back up.

TIPS

Caution!
Be careful of the amount of blur used. Too much blur and the photo will look more surreal than real. Also, watch the edges as you erase. Edges can make or break this effect. Change your brush size and hardness as you go around important edges on your subject. You may also need a selection to protect an important edge.

Try This!
If you want to keep your layers, you can use the merge and copy layers technique discussed in Chapter 5. You need a flattened "photo," but a flattened layer representing that photo will do. Select the top layer and then press Ctrl+Shift+Alt+E (PC) or Cmd+Shift+Opt+E (Mac) to create a merged-flattened layer above it that can be used for this task.

Try This!
You can also make a selection around your subject, feather it appropriately, and then press Delete or Backspace to reveal the background. On some photos, this provides better results than the Eraser technique, especially if the subject has a lot of intricate edge detail. On other photos, making a selection just takes more time, and the Eraser technique is more efficient and effective.

Remove
DISTRACTING COLORS

Color is important for most photographs. Color is not, however, arbitrary and constant. Any color is influenced by other colors around it, dark or bright areas near it, people's feelings about it, and how a particular sensor and camera deal with it. Colors are never a constant.

When you have a distracting color within the image area, it can detract from your picture. This probably happens most commonly with red. Red is a dominant color and draws the viewer's eye away from other parts of the picture. This is especially true if the subject does not have bright colors that can compete with it. Other colors can be a problem, too, when they are bright and saturated and draw attention away from the focus of the photo. Removing, or at least toning down, problem colors can be an important adjustment for your photograph.

① Click the Adjustment Layer icon in the Layers palette.

② Select Hue/Saturation.

A Hue/Saturation adjustment layer is added to the picture and an adjustment panel is opened.

③ Click the color drop-down menu arrow.

④ Select the color that most closely matches the color you want to change in your photograph.

⑤ Click the first eyedropper.

⑥ Position your cursor over that color in the picture and click the color to refine the Hue/Saturation adjustment limits.

7 Adjust the Hue, Saturation, and Lightness sliders until the color becomes less dominant in the picture.

Usually, the Saturation slider provides the greatest change, but try them all.

#68

8 Press Ctrl/Cmd+I to invert the white layer mask to black.

9 Click the Paintbrush tool.

10 Change the foreground color to white.

11 Paint white over the problem color area.

This enables you to limit the color adjustment to only one part of the picture.

TIPS

Did You Know?

You can change the layer mask between black and white in a couple of ways. One is to press Ctrl/Cmd+I to invert a color mask from white to black or black to white. Another is to click the Edit menu and then select Fill Layer to completely fill the layer mask with black or white, which replaces any work done in the layer mask.

Try This!

Use this technique to tone down a color in the background of your photograph that cannot be removed any other way. You may find that you cannot crop that color out nor can you blur it without adversely affecting the rest of the picture. Yet, by simply toning it down, you make it less dominant.

Try This!

If several colors are giving you problems, use a separate adjustment layer for each one. Although it is possible to do more than one color with a single adjustment layer, that can be confusing. Using single layers for each color makes it easy to go to the exact layer needed for any adjustment. Name your layers by the color affected.

Improve
BLANK SKIES

During the day, skies are bright. Typically, they are much brighter than anything on the ground. If you try to photograph the sky so that it has good color, you usually end up with a silhouette for a subject. If you expose to get good detail in the subject, then the sky becomes blank, or white. Another problem occurs when photographing on days with a hazy sky. The sky often looks blank in the photograph then, as well.

You could select the sky and simply fill it with a blue. This usually does not look very good, even to the point of looking quite artificial. Skies are not a consistent shade of blue. They are darker higher in the sky, and get lighter closer to the horizon. You need to duplicate this when fixing a blank sky so that it looks right.

① Click the Magic Wand selection tool.

② Click the sky to select it.

   Shift+click multiple times to get all the sky.

③ Click the New Layer icon in the Layers palette to add a blank layer.

④ Rename your layer **Fix sky**.

⑤ Click Select and choose Refine Edge.

   The Refine Edge dialog box appears.

⑥ Click the red icon to create an overlay to better show the edges of your selection.

⑦ Adjust the Smooth, Feather, and Contract/Expand sliders until the edges along the sky look good.

⑧ Click OK.

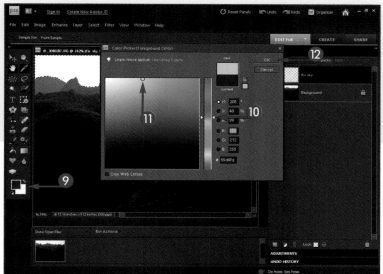

9 Click the foreground color to get the Color Picker (Foreground Color) dialog box.

10 Click the center color bar to pick a good sky-blue color.

11 Click in the big color box to refine your color selection.

12 Click OK.

69

DIFFICULTY LEVEL

13 Click the background color to get the Color Picker (Background Color) dialog box.

14 Click the center color bar to pick a good sky-blue color.

15 Click in the big color box to get a color lighter than the foreground color.

16 Click OK.

TIPS

Did You Know?

Refine Edge is a useful control in Photoshop Elements for refining a selection edge. All the controls in Refine Edge have long been available in Photoshop Elements, but before Photoshop Elements 7 they were not so convenient or accessible. Being able to add an overlay that clearly shows what edges will look like based on the selection is also a great benefit.

Try This!

When you deal with skies that are broken up by the subject, by trees in the background, and other pictorial objects, you may find it helpful to use the Magic Wand selection tool with Contiguous unselected. This enables the program to look for the sky throughout the picture even if it is not directly connected to the area that you click on.

Did You Know?

The Color Picker that appears when you click the foreground or background color enables you to choose all sorts of colors. The central color bar is for selecting hue, and the large box enables you to select the brightness of a color from left to right and the saturation from top to bottom.

Improve
BLANK SKIES

Placing a sky fix in a separate layer over your picture has several advantages. It enables you to change and tweak the sky as much as you want without affecting the underlying picture. In addition, it enables you to tone down the intensity of the fixed colors by simply modifying the Opacity of the layer. You can also change the color of the sky by using Hue/Saturation on the layer.

Finally, a separate layer is very important because it enables you to add noise to the fixed sky. All photographs have some sort of noise at some level. When Photoshop Elements adds color, it adds it in a pure form, without any noise whatsoever. This can make the sky look unnatural, even though a real sky has no noise. You need to add some noise to the sky fix so that it matches the rest of the photograph.

⑰ Click the Gradient tool.

⑱ Click high in the sky to start the gradient.

⑲ Drag your cursor down to the bottom of the sky and release to end the gradient.

A new sky appears; it will usually be too intense.

⑳ Deselect your selection by pressing the Esc key.

21 Adjust the Opacity of the sky layer until the sky looks natural.

22 Click the Zoom tool or magnifier, and then click the photo to enlarge a small section of sky in the original photo.

23 Click the Hand tool, and then click and drag your photo to get a good view of both the noise in the original photo and the new sky.

24 Click Filter, select Noise, and then select Add Noise.

● The Add Noise dialog box opens.

25 Add a small amount of noise so the sky is a closer match to the original photo.

26 Click OK.

TIPS

Caution!

Be sure you are in the right layer when you add the sky. You do not want to add the sky to the original image or to any other layer that you might be using. This will cause you problems, although if you accidentally put the sky in the wrong place, you can undo it using the Undo History palette.

Try This!

Often you will find that it takes several tries with the Gradient tool to get a good-looking gradient for sky. You may find that one time the sky looks crooked, another time it does not seem to match the way the rest of the scene looks, and another time the blend is too high or too low. Keep trying the tool until the sky looks good.

More Options!

The Gradient tool has a number of options in the options bar. Most photographers use this tool at its default settings. However, you can choose some other interesting gradients in the options bar. You might like experimenting with them for special-effect purposes. Use the Reset Tool function at the far left to get back to the defaults.

CREATE THE FOCUS
with Gaussian Blur

Photographs look their best when the image is clearly structured for the viewer. You want the viewer to be able to understand what your picture is about or at least understand your interpretation of the scene. Composition, filters, depth of field, and other shooting techniques are used to help define and structure the picture so that it affects the viewer.

A trendy effect photographers have been using for this purpose is a unique use of sharpness. By using special lenses, they create a small area of sharpness within the picture to define exactly what it is they want the viewer to look at. You can do something similar in Photoshop Elements. You create a blur over most of the picture that blends nicely to a sharp area. By choosing this sharp area carefully, you create a strong way of communicating your focus to your viewer.

① Make a selection around a key part of your subject.

② Click Select and choose Feather.

③ Feather the selection by at least 80 pixels.

④ Click Select.

⑤ Choose Inverse to invert the selection.

6 Press Ctrl/Cmd+J to copy the selected area to a new layer.

● You will see a layer with a hole in it over your original image.

7 Click Filter, select Blur, and select Gaussian Blur.

● The Gaussian Blur dialog box opens.

8 Click and drag the Radius slider until you get a nice blurred effect on the top layer.

9 Click OK.

The hole in the top layer enables the sharp photo underneath to show through only in that area.

TIPS

Try This!

You can refine your final picture by using the Eraser tool. Choose a soft-edged brush for the eraser and erase parts of the top blurred layer. Press Ctrl/Cmd+Z to undo anything you do not like. You can also change the Opacity of the eraser to get a more blended effect as you erase an edge.

Did You Know?

A checkerboard pattern on a layer thumbnail in the Layers palette shows you that no pixels are there. This pattern occurs only on pixel layers. This can help you know when a layer has holes or gaps in it so that you can choose the right layer to work on. It also gives you an idea of the shape of the hole.

Try This!

If you are having trouble finding the edge of a layer's pixels as you erase on that layer, try turning off the layer below it. Click the Eye icon to turn the layer off; that way you see only the layer you are working on. A checkerboard pattern shows up where the pixels are gone.

ADD A NEW BACKGROUND
for your subject

How often have you taken a picture of friends or family, and you have liked the subject but not the background? This happens all the time. Sometimes the liveliest photos that really give an interesting interpretation of the person are captured informally, even spur of the moment, with a point-and-shoot camera. In these situations, you rarely have the chance to choose a great background for your subject.

It is possible to change the background in Photoshop Elements. You can create everything from a very simple background to something with rich texture and color. You can even put your subject in front of a totally different real-world background. The technique is the same for both types of backgrounds. Changing backgrounds lets you practice your selection skills and your use of layers. The possibilities are endless and can keep you up late at night trying them all out!

① Copy your photograph to two new layers by pressing Ctrl/Cmd+J twice.

② Pick an interesting foreground color by clicking it and using the Color Picker (Foreground Color) dialog box.

③ Click the middle layer to make it active.

④ Click Edit and then select Fill Layer.

⑤ Click the Contents Use drop-down menu and select Foreground Color.

⑥ Click OK.

● The middle layer is now the same as your foreground color.

You cannot see this color in the actual picture because another layer, a copy of the original image, is covering the second layer.

7 Make a selection around your subject using whichever selection tools work best.

Sometimes you will get the best results by selecting the background and inverting the selection.

8 Click Select and then choose Refine Edge.

The Refine Edge dialog box opens.

9 Click the Red icon to get an overlay that better displays the edge.

10 Use the Zoom and Hand tools as needed to magnify the image and move it around so you can better see the edge.

The Zoom tool zooms in by default. Holding down the Alt or Opt key plus the Zoom tool will zoom out.

11 Adjust the Smooth, Feather, and Contract/Expand sliders to refine the edge of the selection.

12 Click OK.

TIPS

Important!
Watch those edges as you go around your subject. The selection edge really has a big impact on how well the background works with your subject. Select your subject using whichever selection tools work best for you and the subject. Add to and subtract from that selection by pressing the Shift and Alt or Opt keys.

Did You Know?
The red overlay that appears when you use the overlay button in Refine Edge helps you see changes in the selection edge. The red is where nothing is selected; you clearly see the selected area that has no red. This edge shows blending, feathering, and so on, which is not visible with the normal selection edge.

Try This!
Once you start putting backgrounds behind your subject, be aware of sharpness. Normally you will want your subject to be sharp and the background to be less sharp. Because the background is new, you can blur it as much as you want with Gaussian Blur. Usually you want to have at least a slight blur on that new background.

ADD A NEW BACKGROUND
for your subject

So what can you put as a new background for your subject? Bright colors work great with young people. Muted colors work well with gentle portraits. Textures give dimension to a background, and Photoshop Elements offers a lot of them if you experiment with the filters in the Filter menu.

You can open a totally different photograph and use it for a background. An easy way to do this is to make a new layer in that photo pressing Ctrl/Cmd+J, and

then select the Move tool at the upper left of the toolbox. Click the layer and drag it to the photograph of your subject that needs a new background. Be sure that your cursor has gone completely over the edges of the photograph and then release the mouse button. This picture is dropped onto your picture, over the active layer. Move it around with the Move tool, and then blur it so that it looks more natural.

⑬ Click the top layer to be sure it is active.

⑭ Press Delete or Backspace.

The selected area is removed from the top layer and the new background shows through.

⑮ If the edges need improvement, press Ctrl/Cmd and then click the top layer.

This selects the subject.

⑯ Press Ctrl/Cmd+Shift+I to invert the selection.

⑰ Click Select, choose Modify, and then choose Expand.

● The Expand Selection dialog box opens.

⑱ Type a low number of pixels.

⑲ Click OK.

#71 CONTINUED

20 Click Select and choose Feather.

● The Feather Selection dialog box opens.

21 Type a low number of pixels, the same number or one less than you used in the Expand Selection dialog box.

22 Click OK.

23 Click the Eraser tool.

24 Choose a brush size appropriate for the size of your edges.

25 Choose a soft-edged brush.

26 Press Ctrl/Cmd+H to hide the selection edge.

27 Erase along the edge of your subject wherever there are problems.

You can only erase along the edge of the selection.

TIPS

More Options!
Once you have dragged a real photograph onto your picture for a new background, you can also drag it below your subject if the new layer comes into the Layers palette on top. To resize this picture layer, click the Image menu, and then select Resize and then Scale. You then simply drag the sides, top, bottom, and corners in and out as needed.

Try This!
Freely experiment with backgrounds. You can discover all sorts of backgrounds by using different colors and different images, and then just trying a lot of filters in the Filter menu. You can even copy your original picture below your subject and apply filters to that layer just for the effect.

Try This!
Look for backgrounds that complement your subject. Sure, you can put a subject against some wacky background, but if the light, contrast, and tonality of your subject do not go with that background, the picture will never look right. It will look like the subject and background were pasted against each other.

Size and Sharpen Photos

Digital photos have to be sized for specific uses. They are not like film. With film, you simply put the negative into an enlarger and make the picture bigger or smaller as needed. You cannot do that with a digital photo. For example, once a picture is resized to a small image, that small image cannot be resized with any quality to a big one.

In general, do all of your processing work on a photograph using a master Photoshop or PSD (Photoshop Document) file. Then save that master file for any future resizing purposes. The best way to do this is to create a new file for every new size of picture you need. You do not want to resize your master file, and then save over this version because you will not be able to get back to the original size from the saved file.

Some photographers will resize an image for every small change in size that they need. This is rarely needed. You will not find a lot of quality difference changing from an 8×10-inch photo to a 5×7-inch photo, for example. But you will see a difference if you try to use an 8×10-inch photo for a 2×3-inch wallet-size image or vice versa.

Top 100

BASIC WORKFLOW
for image sizing

Photoshop Elements puts the key photo-sizing controls in one place: Image Size under Resize in the Image menu. To use the image-sizing options effectively, it helps to understand how Photoshop Elements structures the resizing of an image. You can make a picture bigger or smaller by either changing how many pixels are in a picture or by changing the spacing of the pixels that are in an image file. You can also size a layered or flattened file.

The program uses some rather complex algorithms to make an image file bigger or smaller in pixels, yet retain the best possible quality for the picture. You have to tell Photoshop Elements how to handle your particular picture, which is what the options in Image Size enable you to do. The right choices are fairly straightforward; however, there are options that can create problems if you mischoose them. This should not deter you, but you do need to pay attention to what you are doing.

① Click Image.

② Select Resize.

③ Select Image Size.

The Image Size dialog box opens.

④ Be sure Resample Image is unselected.

⑤ Type either the Width or Height and the other dimension appears automatically.

● Resolution changes because at this point you are only moving pixels closer together or farther apart.

● Pixel Dimensions do not change because there are no new pixels.

⑥ Select Resample Image (☐ changes to ☑).

This tells the program to add or subtract pixels to change an image size.

⑦ Type a Resolution.

⑧ Type a new width or height.

● Pixel Dimensions change because new pixels will be created.

⑨ Click the box below Resample Image.

⑩ Select Bicubic Smoother if your photograph will be enlarged; that is, Pixel Dimensions increase.

Select Bicubic Sharper if your photograph will be reduced in size.

⑪ Click OK to resize the picture.

TIPS

Did you know?
Image sizing is not designed to give you a specific size such as 8×10 inches or 11×14 inches. It is designed to make your overall picture larger or smaller. If you want a very specific size, you need to use Image Size to get a correct height or width, and then use the Crop tool to get the final size.

Caution!
In general, you will always leave the Constrain Proportions box checked. This means your picture will be resized according to the original proportions of the photograph. If this box is unchecked, you will get wildly distorted photographs from your resizing.

Did You Know?
When you enlarge an image size and pixels are created, the differences between those pixels must be smoothed out so your photo has maximum quality. That is why you use Bicubic Smoother. When you reduce the size of an image, detail is thrown out but you want to retain the sharpest detail. That is why you use Bicubic Sharper.

Size photos
FOR PRINTING

Inkjet printers do a fantastic job creating superb photo quality for your prints. But to get the optimum quality, the image file must be sized properly for a given print output size. You will not get the best results if you simply print any and all image sizes from one master file that has a specific size and resolution. In fact, print image quality can decline from too little or too much resolution.

Resolution is a very important part of image sizing for a print. You need to create an image with a printing resolution. All inkjet printers will create a high-quality print using resolutions between 200 and 360 ppi (pixels per inch). If you can resize your image without resampling the picture and stay within this range, you can use your master image file for printing. You do not need to make and save new copies of this image until you start resampling the picture.

1 Click Image.

2 Select Resize.

3 Select Image Size.

● The Image Size dialog box opens.

4 Be sure Resample Image is unselected.

5 Type **200** for Resolution.

6 Note the width and height as this is the maximum size for printing without resampling.

⑦ Type **360** for Resolution.

⑧ Note the width and height as this is the minimum size for printing without resampling.

You now know how big or small you can print without increasing or decreasing the number of pixels.

⑨ Select Resample Image when you want to change the size of your picture beyond the range represented by 200 to 360 ppi (☐ changes to ☑).

Use 200 ppi for bigger pictures and 360 ppi for smaller pictures.

⑩ Choose Bicubic Smoother if your photograph will be enlarged, that is, Pixel Dimensions increase.

Choose Bicubic Sharper if your photograph will be reduced in size.

⑪ Click OK to resize the picture.

TIPS

Important!
The resolution of an image is not the same thing as the resolution of a printer. Image resolution refers to the way pixels create tones and details in a photo. Printer resolution has to do with how ink droplets are put down on the paper by the printer. They mean very different things.

Did You Know?
Pixels per inch, or ppi, is a standard way of measuring the density of pixels in a picture, which is also a measure of resolution. Pixels alone are not enough information. To understand resolution, you must have pixels combined with inches, which is an indication of how many pixels fit in a linear dimension.

Did You Know?
The type of paper used for printing affects the ppi needed in the original image. Matte finishes can handle lower resolutions quite nicely, while glossy papers tend to require higher resolutions. Do your own tests and see how resolution affects the look of an image on the papers that you use.

Size photos
FOR E-MAIL

Sharing photos via e-mail is a great way to get your pictures in front of friends, family, and others. You can, for example, take pictures of your kids playing soccer in the afternoon, and then send off copies of those pictures to the grandparents that night. Even if the grandparents live nearby, this is not possible with film.

However, a common problem with e-mail pictures occurs when people simply download the image files from the camera and send them attached to an e-mail. The high megapixel cameras of today have quite sizable files, even when using JPEG. This can cause problems for the recipient of the e-mail. Files this size can take too long for recipients to download or even crash their e-mail software. You can avoid this problem by sizing your pictures properly for e-mail purposes.

1 Click Image.

2 Select Resize.

3 Select Image Size.

● The Image Size dialog box opens.

4 Select Resample Image
(☐ changes to ☑).

5 Type **100** for Resolution.

6 Type **8** for the longest side, whether it is width or height.

This creates a good, small image file for standard e-mailing purposes.

⑦ Type **150** for Resolution.

⑧ Type **8** for the longest side, whether it is width or height.

This creates a small image file that can be both e-mailed and printed.

⑨ Click OK.

Your image now appears smaller in size in the Photoshop Elements workspace.

Make it fill the workspace again by pressing Ctrl/Cmd+0.

⑩ Click File and select Save As.

● The JPEG Options dialog box appears.

⑪ Select JPEG for the file format.

⑫ Click and drag the Quality slider to set a moderate JPEG Quality setting between 6 and 9.

⑬ Click OK.

TIPS

Did You Know?

A resolution of 100 ppi is easy to remember and works fine for displaying pictures that have been sent by e-mail. Few monitors display at 72 ppi anymore, which used to be the recommended resolution for e-mail.

Did You Know?

For optimum printing quality, you will generally choose a resolution of at least 200 ppi. However, 150 ppi will give an acceptable, photo-quality print while at the same time enabling you to have a significantly smaller image size for e-mailing.

More Options!

When you save an image as a new JPEG file, a dialog box with options for JPEG settings appears. As you change the Quality setting, you will see a number appear below the Preview check box. This number is the size of your image based on the Quality setting you selected. For e-mail, Quality numbers between 6 and 9 are common and work fine. Look for a setting that provides a final file size that is less than 200KB (the number appears below the Preview check box).

SHARPEN PHOTOS
with Unsharp Mask

You can only sharpen pixels in Photoshop Elements. This means you must sharpen a flattened file that is saved for a specific purpose or use a technique that creates a pixel-based layer for sharpening.

Sharpening in Photoshop Elements is designed to get the optimum amount of sharpness from your original image based on a sharp picture to begin with. It will not help blurred or out-of-focus pictures.

For a variety of reasons, images coming from a digital sensor are not optimally sharp. Most cameras apply

some sharpening to a JPEG file as it is processed inside the camera. No sharpening is applied to a RAW file. Yet, no matter what image comes into Photoshop Elements, it usually needs some degree of sharpening. Unsharp Mask is a good tool for sharpening. The name comes from a traditional process used to sharpen photos for printing plates in the commercial printing industry. It is not about making unsharp pictures sharp.

① Click Enhance.

② Select Unsharp Mask.

● The Unsharp Mask dialog box opens.

③ Type a number between 130 and 180 for Amount.

Amount is the intensity of the sharpening.

Different subjects need levels of sharpening appropriate to their look.

4 Type a number between 1.0 and 1.5 for Radius.

Radius affects how sharpness is enhanced around an edge.

Be careful of overdoing this control — watch for unnatural halos of brightness around contrasted edges.

5 Type a number between 3 and 6 for Threshold.

Threshold affects how small details such as noise are sharpened.

Set this higher for images showing more noise, and lower for those showing less.

6 Click OK.

TIPS

Caution!

Beware of oversharpening. While you can increase the Amount and Radius to make a blurry picture look sort of sharp or make sharpness look intense, this can also damage your photo in a lot of ways. It will make tonalities look harsh, and you will lose fine tones and colors in the picture.

More Options!

The Preview window in the Unsharp Mask dialog box can be very helpful. Click part of the picture to show its detail in the preview. Click on and off the preview picture to see how sharpening is being applied. Click the preview picture and drag to move its position around so it displays key sharp parts of the image.

More Options!

Change your sharpening based on the subject. Landscapes and architecture typically do well with higher sharpening numbers for Amount and Radius. Photos of people, especially close-ups of faces, usually need less sharpening, even as low as 100 for Amount and less than 1 for Radius.

SHARPEN PHOTOS
with Adjust Sharpness

Adjust Sharpness is a newer addition to Photoshop Elements for sharpening opposed to Unsharp Mask. Adjust Sharpness uses advanced algorithms for sharpening to get the maximum detail possible from a photograph. You might wonder why you would not use this way to sharpen photos all the time. The reason is because of noise and Threshold.

Adjust Sharpness does not have a Threshold control. This means if you have noise in your picture, that

noise is likely to be sharpened just as much as anything else in the picture. As a result, the noise becomes more visible. It certainly does not hurt to try Adjust Sharpness. If noise shows up too much from that, then go back to Unsharp Mask.

Adjust Sharpness works well for highly detailed pictures, such as landscapes and architecture, but when you need more gentle sharpening, such as with people, you may find Unsharp Mask works better.

① Click Enhance.

② Select Adjust Sharpness.

The Adjust Sharpness dialog box opens.

③ Select More Refined (☐ changes to ☑).

④ Click and drag the preview window until you find a good place to check sharpness.

Alternately, click your cursor on something that should be sharp in the photo itself.

5 Type a number between 100 and 160 for Amount.

Amount is slightly different than Amount in Unsharp Mask.

DIFFICULTY LEVEL

6 Type a number between 1.0 and 1.5 for Radius.

Radius is also slightly different from Radius in Unsharp Mask.

7 Click OK.

 TIPS

Important!

Because noise can become more obvious in Adjust Sharpness, it is important to look for it. Enlarge the picture in the Preview window by clicking the plus button underneath the Preview window. Check areas such as dark parts of an image that have been brightened and the sky. They usually show noise before other areas.

More Options!

The Remove box instructs Adjust Sharpen how to handle sharpness. Click it and a drop-down menu appears. Sometimes it is easier to sharpen pictures with motion blur by selecting Motion Blur. And sometimes you can get sharper pictures with an out-of-focus subject by selecting Lens Blur.

More Options!

If you read anything about Photoshop and Photoshop Elements, you will find a variety of formulas for Unsharp Mask and Adjust Sharpness. Generally, they all work and can be worth a try. Every photographer will use different formulas because sharpness truly depends on the subject and on the personal tastes of the photographer.

Sharpen photos
WHEN YOU HAVE LAYERS

The sharpening features of Photoshop Elements must have pixels to work on. This presents a challenge when you are working with layers because first, you need to have pixels in a layer in order to sharpen it, and second, even if you do have pixels in a layer, you can only sharpen one layer at a time. Once you have finished working on a photograph using layers, you normally will sharpen the whole picture, including everything that adjustment layers might do to it.

The way to do this is to create a special layer on top of all your other layers that merges those layers together into one pixel layer. You then sharpen this layer. Label it the sharpened layer so you know what it is. You can later go back and adjust anything underneath that layer, although you will need to create a new sharpened layer if you do.

① Click the top layer.

② Press Alt+Ctrl+Shift+E for the PC and Opt+Cmd+Shift+E for the Mac.

You are pressing the modifier keys plus E.

● A new layer formed from a copy of the merged layers appears at the top of the layer stack.

③ Rename this layer **SharpenedLayer**.

4 Click Enhance, and then select Unsharp Mask.

● The Unsharp Mask dialog box opens.

5 Type a number between 130 and 180 for Amount.

6 Type a number between 1.0 and 1.5 for Radius.

7 Type a number between 3 and 6 for Threshold.

8 Click OK.

● The layer named Sharpened Layer is now sharpened, but nothing else in the photo is sharpened.

TIPS

Did You Know?

Unsharp Mask can be very useful when you are sharpening the layer created from merged layers in a many-layered file. When a lot of adjustment layers are applied to a photograph, especially a JPEG picture, you will find noise and other image artifacts begin to appear. You can minimize them using a Threshold setting, which does not exist in Adjust Sharpness.

Did You Know?

The merge and make new layer command, Alt+Ctrl+Shift+E for the PC or Opt+Cmd+Shift+E for the Mac, is a fairly well-known command in the Photoshop world. However, it does not show up in any menus. You have to know it exists and what it does in order to use it. This command is the same in both Photoshop and Photoshop Elements. Be very careful that you click the top layer before using the command.

Caution!

If you are shooting JPEG, be very wary of oversharpening your photo. Many cameras already apply a high amount of sharpening on their JPEG files, especially lower-priced cameras. Watch out for gentle, pleasant tonalities becoming harsh and unpleasant.

SELECTIVELY SHARPEN
parts of your photo

If you have a photograph with a close-up of a flower, and that flower is sharp while the background is out of focus, you only really need to sharpen the flower. If you have a portrait with an out-of-focus background, the face needs to be sharp, but not the background.

In fact, there are good reasons that you do not want to try sharpening out-of-focus areas at all. A big reason is noise. Noise tends to show up more in out-of-focus areas and does not need to be sharpened. Another reason is that odd little details can be sharpened in the out-of-focus area, degrading the visual quality of the area. If you restrict your sharpness to only the areas that need to be sharp, you will not have these problems. Selectively sharpening is only for pictures with a distinct difference in sharpness between the subject and the rest of the image.

① Press Ctrl/Cmd+J to duplicate your photo to a new layer.

② Alternately, click on the top layer of a layered file, and then press Alt+Ctrl+Shift+E or Opt+Cmd+Shift+E.

③ Click Enhance, and then select Unsharp Mask.

● The Unsharp Mask dialog box opens.

④ Type a number between 130 and 180 for Amount.

⑤ Type a number between 1.0 and 1.5 for Radius.

⑥ Type a number between 3 and 6 for Threshold.

⑦ Click OK.

8 Click the Eraser tool in the toolbox.

9 Use a large, soft-edged brush to start.

10 Click the Eye icon for the bottom layer, Background, to turn it off.

11 Begin to erase the parts of the picture that are not sharp.

By turning off the bottom layer, you can more easily see what you are erasing.

Change your brush size as needed to go around your sharp subject, and press Ctrl/Cmd+Z to undo any mistakes.

12 Click the Eye icon for the bottom layer, Background, to turn it back on.

The top layer is now a sharpened layer, but only where the original picture was sharp.

TIPS

Caution!
Be wary of using high Threshold numbers. Threshold is very useful in minimizing the impact of sharpening on noise and other image detail problems called artifacts. But it can also affect small important detail. Keep your Threshold setting below 6 when you can, and only go up to a maximum of 12.

Did You Know?
You typically do sharpening at the end, or at least toward the end, of your image processing workflow. The reason is that sharpening affects things like noise and other details that can be changed as you process the image. Sharpening too early can cause problems with these things.

Attention!
Think about your subject as you sharpen your photograph. Sharpening is not a one-size-fits-all adjustment. Some subjects look great with high sharpness, such as rocky landscapes. Others look better with lower amounts of sharpness, such as peoples' faces.

Go Beyond the Basics

Once you have mastered the basics of working on images, you may want to look for other things to do with your pictures. One option is to convert your pictures to black-and-white. It was not all that long ago that color was the special type of photography and black-and-white was rather ordinary. At that time, black-and-white was commonly seen in every publication. Today, color is the most common way that pictures are printed. Black-and-white has become a very special way of dealing with pictures, giving images a unique look in contrast to very common color photos. In addition, black-and-white gives you multiple ways to deal with a subject.

Another fun thing you can do with digital photography and Photoshop Elements is create a panoramic photograph. This type of photograph is created from a series of images. The width or height of the scene is too great for your lens to include when you are shooting, so you make up for it by taking pictures across the scene. Alternately, you may like the format of a panoramic image, but want a photograph that is bigger than possible from simply cropping a panoramic format from a single image. Photoshop Elements supports the multi-image panoramic quite well.

Top 100

Convert color photos to
BLACK-AND-WHITE

With many digital cameras, you can set the camera to take a black-and-white photograph. The advantage to this is that you are able to see exactly what you get from a scene when it is turned into black-and-white. The disadvantage is that the black-and-white image is locked into a JPEG file and cannot be changed.

Any black-and-white photo is created by changing the colors of the world into tones of black-and-white. When you convert a color image to black-and-white in

Photoshop Elements, you have a lot of control over how the colors change into tones of black-and-white. This can be an extremely important way to work because sometimes colors that stand out in a color image blend together when they are turned into black-and-white equivalents. Because you can change how this conversion occurs in the computer, you have a lot of power and flexibility when working with black-and-white.

First, process the color image as you normally would.

① Click Enhance.

② Select Convert to Black and White.

● The Convert to Black and White dialog box opens.

③ Compare the color and black-and-white images to see if you like the interpretation of the scene.

④ Click on different styles, or interpretations, of conversions and see how they work with your photo.

⑤ Modify a style by changing the brightness of tones by adjusting the intensity of colors.

⑥ Click OK.

TIPS

Important!

The default black-and-white conversion of your image by Photoshop Elements should be seen purely as a starting point. Sometimes it will look fine, but most of the time you will need to, at least, adjust the color sliders to refine how colors are changed into tones of gray.

Did You Know?

Strong adjustments to a picture as it is converted to a black-and-white image can cause some undesirable effects. Watch out for noise appearing in areas that have had an extreme change. Also beware of breaks in the tonality, which will look like steps of tones, in smooth toned areas such as skies.

Did You Know?

RAW files always come into Camera Raw in Photoshop Elements as color images even if you shot them as black-and-white in the camera. One advantage to RAW for black-and-white is you are able to use a 16-bit file. This allows for stronger tonal adjustments without breaks in smooth toned areas.

Adjust your photos in
BLACK-AND-WHITE

The tonalities and gradations of grays are what bring a black-and-white image to life. This is why these tonalities and gradations are very important. The first way to get them is when you make the conversion from color to black-and-white. Sometimes your picture looks great at this point.

Often, however, you need to do more using the controls that have been discussed in the rest of this book. Because a good, strong black is very important to a good-looking black-and-white image, it can be

very helpful to reexamine the blacks in your photograph. You may want to set them to a higher point within the range of dark grays for a dramatic effect. Midtones are also very important, so you may want to use Color Curves to see various effects. All black-and-white images are interpretations of the world because humans do not see the world this way. Your interpretation is important and is affected by these adjustments.

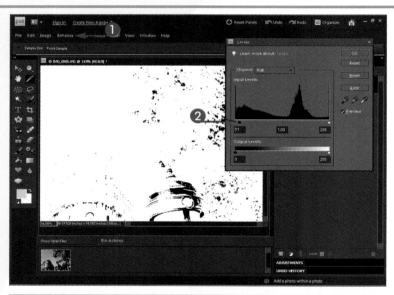

① Click Enhance, select Adjust Lighting, and then select Levels.

② Press the Alt/Opt key as you move the black slider toward the right until you like how your blacks look.

You can also do this using a Levels adjustment layer.

③ Click Enhance, select Adjust Color, and then select Adjust Color Curves.

● The Adjust Color Curves dialog box appears.

④ Adjust the shadow, midtone, and highlight tones until you like the overall brightness of the picture and how the tonalities look.

5 Examine your photo for tonal imbalances or areas that should be darker.

6 Click the Adjustment Layer icon and select Brightness/Contrast.

7 Adjust Brightness to darken the picture.

8 Press Ctrl/Cmd+I to invert the layer mask to black and block the darkening effect.

9 Use a soft white paintbrush to brush in the darkening where needed in the picture.

TIPS

Important!

Grayscale and Remove Color are two additional black-and-white adjustments in Photoshop Elements. They are not recommended for most black-and-white conversions because they change color to black-and-white tones in one, and only one, way. You cannot change this.

Did You Know?

You will sometimes hear black-and-white images called grayscale. Grayscale is a term that simply refers to the way an image deals with color, in this case a scale of gray tones. The term tends to be used more by computer people than photographers.

Did You Know?

Another term for black-and-white is *monochrome*. While this is somewhat trendy, monochrome actually refers to any image based on one color. It is not limited to gray and can include red, blue, or any other color.

Create
TONED IMAGES

One of the classic ways photographers work with black-and-white images was to tone them. This meant adding a slight color to a black-and-white image. The most common toning color was a warm tone called sepia tone. Another common toning color was a slight blue for a cool effect.

Toning can be an effective way to enrich your black-and-white images. You have a whole range of possibilities here, from a subtle effect that provides a hint of color to the picture to a strongly colored effect for special purposes. One advantage of a toned image is that it usually prints very nicely on any inkjet printer as compared to a pure black-and-white photo.

Photographers will sometimes create dramatic posters using a strongly colored black-and-white image. For this sort of effect, they often create rather dramatic black areas and white areas in the photograph that go beyond a simple black-and-white conversion.

① Click the Adjustment Layer icon and select Hue/Saturation.

② Select Colorize (☐ changes to ☑).

● The image now has a color and is a monochrome image based on that color.

● For a sepia-toned image, use a number between 35 and 50 points for Hue to get a warm tone you like.

● For a cool-toned image, use a number between 180 and 210 points for Hue.

● In Saturation, use a lower number for a less intense color or a higher number for a more intense color.

● Use the layer Opacity to reduce the effect of the color as needed.

TIPS

More Options!

As you make a color image into a black-and-white photo, you may find it helpful to save different versions of your pictures. An easy way to do this is to select Duplicate in the File menu. This option creates an immediate copy with a new name that is saved to the same folder as your original. Now do the changes to the copy.

Try This!

You can modify the toning effect using layer blending modes. Click the blending modes box called Normal at first, and then try the blending modes grouped under Overlay. Some of them can be pretty extreme, but all of them can create interesting effects with your photograph.

More Options!

Have fun with toning colors. There is no right or wrong, only what you like or dislike. While most black-and-white photographs probably do not look their best with extreme colors, it can be fun to try unexpected colors to create images that are unique and elicit attention for special purposes.

Use the Smart Brush
FOR CREATIVE EFFECTS

You get a fun special effect when you adjust one area of your picture one way and another area completely differently. A good example of this is a photograph with the subject in color, and the background black-and-white. It could also include a very small part of the picture, such as a red rose being held by a young girl, with only the rose in color.

You can do special effects like this with layers: Copy a photo to a layer, apply a unique effect to the top layer, and then in that layer, erase wherever you want to reveal of the original image underneath. You can also literally paint the effect onto your picture using the Smart Brush. The Smart Brush adds an adjustment layer to your photograph, and then uses the Quick Selection tool with the layer mask to smartly place the adjustment where you brush.

① Click the Smart Brush in the toolbox.

② Click the Smart Brush effects icon.

③ Choose the effect that you wish to paint on your picture.

④ Select an appropriate brush size for your photograph.

⑤ Begin painting on the part of the picture where you want the effect to occur.

● A special adjustment layer is added to your photograph.

● Photoshop Elements smartly finds similar areas to use for your effect.

Sometimes the tool selects too much and applies the effect where you do not want it.

 # 82

DIFFICULTY LEVEL

⑥ Change the effect brush to an effect removal brush by clicking the small brush icon in the upper-left corner of your photograph.

⑦ Adjust the brush size to fit the area that you wish to change.

⑧ Click in that area.

It often works better to click in areas to remove in effect, and then brush over the area.

⑨ Press Ctrl/Cmd+H to hide the selection edge so that you can better see what is happening to your picture.

Revise the effect as needed.

⑩ Click the Select menu, and then choose Refine Mask to feather and smooth the edge so the effect blends naturally.

TIPS

Important!

Unless your background is very simple, you will find you must change brush sizes as you use the Smart Brush. A large brush works well at first, but then begins to capture too much of a photograph. When this happens, you will need to switch to a smaller brush. Remember to use the [and] keys to quickly change your brush size.

Try This!

Because everything you do with a Smart Brush uses an adjustment layer plus a layer mask, changes to your picture are not permanent. This means you can freely experiment with the Smart Brush effects. If you do not like something, simply drag the layer to the Trash Can icon to delete it.

More Options!

You can use the Smart Brush to make a lot of interesting adjustments to your picture. They all work the same way in that an effect is applied to your picture in specific areas as you paint over the image. Explore the complete list of Smart Brush choices and you will find a number will probably work with your types of pictures.

Create a
HAND-COLORED LOOK

A classic effect for black-and-white photography was made by taking a black-and-white print and then painting colors by hand onto that print. Most of this was done in a very realistic way, but some of this hand coloring was done in quite unusual ways as well. Either way, it required a bit of an effort to do as you had to have prints made and the right paint for working on the images. If you made a mistake, you had to throw out the print and start all over again.

You can duplicate this effect in Photoshop Elements, yet you do not have to worry about making mistakes and do not need special paints. In addition, you have a great deal of flexibility over the colors you use, and you can change any of them whenever you want. This can be a fun way of creating a striking new look for your photographs.

① Duplicate your photo by pressing Ctrl/Cmd+J.

② Click Enhance.

③ Select Adjust Color, and then select Remove Color.

You now have a black-and-white image on top of a color photo.

④ Click the Adjustment Layer icon to add a blank layer.

⑤ Name that layer based on a color you want to use for the photo.

⑥ Repeat these steps to add as many layers as you think you will need based on the colors you plan to use.

7 Click the Eye icon for the black-and-white layer to turn it off.

8 Click the Eyedropper in the toolbox.

9 Click a color in the picture that you wish to use.

● This color now appears as the foreground color.

10 Click the Eye icon for the black-and-white layer to turn it back on.

83

DIFFICULTY LEVEL

11 Click the layer you want to use for this color.

12 Click the Paintbrush in the toolbox.

13 Choose a good-sized, soft-edged brush.

14 Select Color for the layer blending mode.

15 Paint over the photo where you want this color to appear.

TIPS

Did You Know?

You may wonder if it is better to create the black-and-white layer using Remove Color or by making your own black-and-white adjustment. This is really going to depend on personal taste and individual photographs. There is no right or wrong way to do it.

Try This!

A quick and easy way to get to the Eyedropper tool when you are in any other tool is to simply press the Alt/Opt key. This immediately changes whatever cursor you are using to the Eyedropper. You can then click a color and it will appear in the foreground color; then you release the Alt/Opt key and the original tool returns.

More Options!

It is okay if you do not have the right amount of layers when you get started on this technique. The only reason for adding layers at the beginning is to get you started with a set of layers that will separate your colors. You can add or subtract layers later if your plans change as you work on the image.

Create a
HAND-COLORED LOOK

The hand-colored, or hand-painted, look has a lot of possibilities. There is no one way to use this technique. You can choose realistic colors or you can decide to color your subject and its surroundings in some totally new way. You can make this effect look very pale and pastel by both the choice of your colors and keeping the layers at a low Opacity setting. You can also make this effect look very intense by choosing very saturated colors and keeping the layers at 100% Opacity.

You also do not have to color the entire photograph. Sometimes it can be interesting to only add one or just a few colors to a picture. You can also be as precise in your coloring as you want, but many photographers find that the effect looks quite interesting if the edges are not precise.

16 Click the next layer.

17 Click the foreground color.

● The Color Picker (Foreground Color) dialog box appears.

18 Click a color you would like to use.

19 Click OK.

● The foreground color changes to the selected color.

20 Paint on the new color.

● Be sure the layer blending mode is set to Color.

21 Change the Opacity of the layer until the color looks right.

- Continue this process, layer by layer, until you have finished painting color on your image.

  Use selections if needed to confine color to certain areas.

TIPS

Try This!

You can get the colors you use for painting from two places, as you have seen in this task: from the original picture or from a foreground color. Try both techniques to see which one gives you the colors that best suit your needs and your photograph.

Important!

In this technique, you have been using a separate color layer for each color. It is possible to put more than one color on a layer, but this is not recommended. You are more likely to have problems adjusting colors if you have more than one color on a layer. Keep them separate and you will find that your image work has more flexibility, too.

More Options!

As you paint a color onto your photograph, change the brush size as you go to better match changes within the photograph. In addition, use the Eraser tool at different sizes to remove areas of color that have spilled onto places where you do not want it.

Photograph a scene
FOR A PANORAMIC IMAGE

Digital photography has meant a real increase in the popularity of a panoramic image. The panoramic image is like a wide-screen movie — physically, it is a photo that is very wide compared to its depth. It is possible to crop a photograph to get a panoramic look to an image. In that case, however, your picture can never be very big as it is limited by the maximum size of the image file.

You create a multi-image panoramic photo by shooting two or more images across a scene, and then merging them together in the computer. This type of panoramic shot gives you a very large image because your original image file size is actually quite a bit smaller than the final photo. This means you can make very large prints without any loss in quality. In addition, you can shoot a wider view of the scene than is possible otherwise, including a full 360-degree photograph.

Before taking your panoramic photo, find a scene with distinctive photo elements from the left to right.

1 Find a beginning.

2 Include an interesting middle.

3 Finish with an end.

Next, set up your tripod.

4 Level the top of the tripod below the tripod head.

5 Level the camera.

6 Set your camera to Manual exposure.

Set one exposure for the scene to be used for all images.

84

DIFFICULTY LEVEL

7 Shoot a series of pictures across the scene.

8 Overlap the pictures by 30 to 50 percent so that they can blend well in Photoshop Elements.

TIPS

Try This!

You can do verticals in a panoramic format, as well. This creates a tall, narrow image. The process is the same except that you shoot a series of images that overlap from top to bottom, rather than left to right. This can be a great way to photograph a waterfall, for example.

Important!

Manual exposure, including setting a specific white balance, is very important when you are shooting panoramic images. If you shoot your camera on automatic, you will get variations of exposure among the series of photos you take across the scene. This exposure variation makes the photos much more difficult to blend together.

More Options!

You can do several things to level your tripod and camera. A simple, compact level from the hardware store can help get you started. You can also get a level that fits into your camera's flash hot shoe that will help you level the camera.

MERGE PHOTOS
for a panoramic picture

Now that you have shot your photos, you are ready to merge them in Photoshop Elements. Photoshop Elements has a powerful merge feature called Photomerge. It includes a number of possibilities for your panoramic images.

However, the basics are very simple. You tell Photoshop Elements which pictures to work with. Photoshop Elements then examines those pictures,

comparing the overlapping areas, and aligns the images. This is why it is so important to get a good overlap with your photographs as you take them. The program lines up the images so the overlapped areas match. This is why it is important to level your camera; otherwise, the matched individual pictures will line up crookedly. Finally, Photoshop Elements puts these pictures together as a panoramic image.

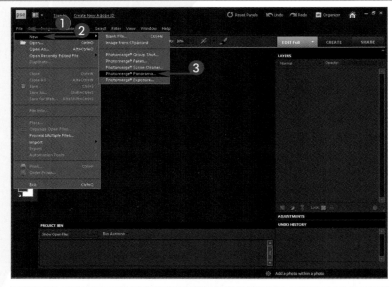

① Click File.

② Select New.

③ Select Photomerge Panorama.

● The Photomerge dialog box opens.

④ Click Browse.

- The Open dialog box opens.

⑤ Select the series of images that make up your panorama.

Click the first one, and then Shift+click the last one and the ones in between are also selected.

⑥ Click Open.

⑦ Select Reposition Only in the Layout area.

⑧ Click OK.

TIPS

Try This!

Sometimes you will find that individual pieces of your panoramic image do not blend together as well as you would like. Because Photoshop Elements puts the individual pictures for a panoramic into layers, you can adjust individual pictures to make them better match the rest. Simply select that area's layer and work on the picture there directly.

Try This!

When is the best time to process individual panoramic images? Before or after putting them into the panorama? There is no simple answer to this. Sometimes it is easier to work on individual pictures before combining them. Other times it is better to work with the individual photos in layers because it gives you a lot of flexibility.

More Options!

When you open Photomerge, you can choose either Folders or Files in the Use drop-down menu. Some photographers will merge a lot of images into one. To keep track of all of them, they often find it easier to put each panorama group into its own folder. This way you can go directly to the folder when you are in Photomerge.

MERGE PHOTOS
for a panoramic picture

Photoshop Elements does most of the work for a panoramic for you. You may discover that the newest aligning and blending algorithms in Photoshop Elements 8 are so good that you need to do little cleanup work. The program offers several different options for putting together your panoramic image. A common look for a panoramic is to use the Reposition Only option. This simply lines up the pictures where they overlap and blends them together in a straightforward manner.

The Perspective option puts the pictures together with perspective effects that make the image look like a bow tie. If you are photographing inside something so that parts of your picture are in front and directly to the sides of you, this option may line things up better. The Cylindrical option maps the image onto imaginary cylinders, which sometimes helps things line up better, especially lines in really wide panoramic shots. The Interactive Layout option requires more work to line up the individual images that make up your panoramic shot.

A panoramic image is created based on your group of photos.

● Each photo is placed into a layer with an automatic layer mask to help blend it with the others.

⑨ Look over your photo to check where the overlap occurs between pictures to see if there are problems that need to be fixed.

⑩ Click the layer mask of a layer that has blending challenges.

⑪ Click the Paintbrush tool.

⑫ Select white for the foreground color.

⑬ Paint over edge areas that need better blending.

Use both white and black colors for the layer mask as needed.

Fix Defects

⑭ Click the Crop tool in the toolbox.

⑮ Click and drag your cursor to create a crop box over the image.

⑯ Press Enter or click the green check mark icon.

#85

CONTINUED

Fix Gaps and Overlap Problems.

⑰ Click the Create new layer icon to add an empty layer over the panoramic.

⑱ Click the Clone Stamp tool in the toolbox.

⑲ Select Sample All Layers in the options toolbar (☐ changes to ☑).

⑳ Select a reasonable brush size to deal with the edge gap on a panoramic image.

Press Alt/Opt and click once to set a clone from a point near the problem area.

㉑ Clone over the gap.

TIPS

Try This!
Sometimes it is hard to see how the edges overlap in the Photomerge output. It can help a lot if you click layers on and off. This helps you to better see edges and what they are doing in your image. You will often find problems with, as well as opportunities for, your image when you do this.

Important!
When your panoramic image is basically complete, you can continue to adjust tonalities and colors. At this point, however, you should adjust them with adjustment layers. An adjustment layer above the top photo in your panoramic image will now adjust the entire panorama. You can limit adjustments to certain layers by using the layer mask.

More Options!
If your photos need quite a bit of work, it can be best to open the individual files first in Photoshop Elements. Here you can adjust the pictures and compare them as you go so they match when they go into the panoramic. Then open Photomerge and simply click the Add Open Files button.

Chapter 8: Go Beyond the Basics 205

Software Plug-ins Make Work Easier

Plug-ins are specialized software programs that "plug into" a larger host program. They offer new features that make the original program more effective or that the host program does not have at all. Nearly all plug-ins that work with Photoshop also work with Photoshop Elements.

One of the big benefits of using a plug-in within Photoshop Elements is that it can expand your efficiency and the power of the program. Many photographers discover that by using a few plug-ins, they can easily create work that is equal to that of more sophisticated photographers using Photoshop. And they can do this at a fraction of the cost of buying Photoshop!

In this chapter, you learn about a variety of plug-ins that offer a range of features for Photoshop Elements users. Few photographers will need or even want all of them. The purpose of this chapter is to give you an idea of what is possible using plug-ins. They do add to the cost of working on images on the computer, but better efficiency and new imaging possibilities can make that cost worthwhile. You can always try out any of the plug-ins discussed here by downloading trial versions from the manufacturers' Web sites. This way you can decide how valuable a given plug-in might be for you at no cost.

Top 100

USE COLOR EFEX PRO
for quick creative adjustments

Nik Software is a company that specializes in plug-ins for photographers. Many plug-ins for Photoshop are really geared more toward designers and creating special effects than the average photographer and his needs. Nik Software creates plug-ins that really seem to speak to photographers' needs.

Color Efex Pro is a plug-in with an entire range of ways to adjust your photograph. They include very direct effects, such as ones to change the brightness balance of certain colors, add a graduated neutral

density filter effect, and get more richness from foliage. They also include adjustments that can fix problems in the picture, such as a dynamic skin softener, a skylight filter, and a white neutralizer. Very creative effects are also included, such as effects that mimic the look of infrared film, create a glamour glow look, and make a pastel image from your original. All of these are in an interface that enables you to see them directly, plus you can control how the effects are applied to the picture.

Note: Plug-ins must be installed before they show up in Photoshop Elements.

① Click Filter.

② Select Nik Software.

③ Select Color Efex Pro.

● The Color Efex Pro plug-in interface appears.

④ Select an effect from the left side.

● The effect appears in the center window.

⑤ Control the effect with the sliders at the upper right.

You can modify the effect by using a control point.

6 Click the Control Points minus button.

7 Click a part of the photo where you want to reduce the effect.

8 Use the sliders associated with the control point to reduce the effect by distance and amount.

9 Click OK.

● The effect is applied to your photograph as a layer.

10 Adjust the intensity of the effect by changing the opacity of the layer.

TIPS

Did You Know?
Control points are a special part of Nik Software programs. They are points you set on your photograph to add or subtract a plug-in effect. They enable you to quickly control where these effects go, without using layer masks.

Did You Know?
Installing most plug-ins is very easy. A plug-in usually comes with an installer that places it in the right folder in your programs on your hard drive. You do need to pay attention because the installer places it here to put the plug-in in Photoshop Elements 8. If it is not, you can tell the installer to put it in the correct place, the Photoshop Elements Plug-Ins folder.

Important!
Most plug-ins must have pixels to work with. This means they need to work on a flattened image file or on a layer made up of pixels. You can apply a plug-in to a layered file by creating a single layer from all of your layers using the keyboard command Ctrl+Shift+Alt+E for the PC or Cmd+Shift+Opt+E for the Mac.

USE COLOR EFEX PRO
for efficient photo work

One thing Nik Software Color Efex Pro does for you is make your work more efficient. You can do many of the adjustments and effects in this plug-in in Photoshop Elements. Color Efex Pro enables you to do these adjustments faster, more easily, and more efficiently.

A good example of this is the Color Efex Graduated Filter. A *graduated filter* can help when you are photographing by balancing the light in a picture. The dark part of the filter keeps bright areas from being too bright. But you cannot always use a graduated filter. And creating a true graduated filter effect in Photoshop Elements can require some tricky work if the original image is too bright or you want some added color. The Color Efex Graduated Filter can quickly change the brightness of one part of the picture plus give it some color as needed. This can be very important when working with skies.

1 Click Filter.

2 Select Nik Software.

3 Select Color Efex Pro.

● The Color Efex Pro plug-in interface appears.

4 Select Graduated Filters from the left side.

● The effect appears in the center window.

5 Click the Color Set drop-down menu.

● A drop-down menu of colors for the effect appears.

You can run your cursor across the colors to see the effects on the photograph.

6 Select a color that works with your subject.

7 Use the Vertical Shift slider first to adjust how high or low the filter effect appears in the photograph.

8 Change the Opacity to make the effect blend with the picture.

9 Adjust the Blend to make the effect blend nicely in the image.

10 Click the Control Points minus button.

11 Click a part of the photo where you want to reduce the effect, such as removing the color from the clouds.

12 Use the sliders associated with the control point to adjust this change.

13 Click OK.

TIPS

Important!

Do your basic image processing before you use a plug-in. You want to be sure that your blacks are set properly, the midtones look good, and the colors are corrected before you start making major changes to the photograph. You must start with a good photograph before using the processing power of a plug-in.

Did You Know?

Color Efex Pro provides three different graduated filter effects. Graduated Filters gives you a choice of colors for the effect. Graduated Neutral Density is purely for darkening part of the picture. Graduated User Defined enables you to pick your own colors for the effect. In addition, Graduated Fog, the special effects filter, applies a fog look.

Check It Out!

You can learn more about Color Efex Pro and other software plug-ins from Nik Software by going to its Web site, www.niksoftware.com. The site has trial versions to download as well as a complete listing of all the features in its programs. Plus you will see some great examples of how the software can be put to work.

REMOVE NOISE
with Dfine

Noise can be a problem with digital photos. Sometimes noise shows up when an underexposed image is brightened to normal levels in Photoshop Elements. Other times it shows up when you need to use a high ISO setting on your camera because of low light levels or when you need a fast shutter speed. Although Photoshop Elements includes some very basic noise reduction controls, they do not work very well when you have the challenge of strong noise in a picture.

For optimum noise reduction, you need a dedicated noise reduction software program. Nik Software Dfine is a plug-in that works to control noise without hurting other detail in the photograph. Dfine also allows you to specifically define areas based on color to determine how much noise reduction you do. This gives you more control over how details are affected.

① Click Filter.

② Select Dfine 2.0.

You may need to magnify the image to see the noise at first, although you can also magnify the image in Dfine.

● Dfine appears.

③ Click Measure Noise.

● Noise is measured at specific areas and reduced.

④ Move your cursor over the image to check the Loupe to see what noise reduction has occurred.

5 Click the Method drop-down menu if more noise reduction is needed and choose Manual.

6 Click the add rectangle button below Manual.

7 Draw a rectangle over an area with a noise problem.

8 Click Measure Noise.

 # 88

9 Click Reduce.

10 Click the Method drop-down menu and select Color Ranges.

11 Click an eyedropper next to a color.

12 Click a color in the photograph that you want to affect.

13 Adjust the slider to change how much noise reduction is done for that color.

14 Repeat steps 11 to 13 for other important colors.

15 Click OK.

TIPS

Important!

Use the Loupe to watch small detail and see how the noise reduction affects it. Noise is essentially small detail. Dfine does a good job of controlling noise without hurting small detail, but sometimes it has trouble telling the difference. Reduce the amount of noise reduction when this happens.

Did You Know?

It can help to take noise reduction off of blacks and very dark parts of the picture. These areas often create a certain structure for sharpness and a slight bit of noise in them can actually help. As long as these areas remain dark in your processing, noise will probably not be a problem.

More Options!

Nik Software includes a number of views of how your picture is being affected. On the left in the upper toolbar, you will see Views with several icons. The first shows you the picture as it is changed. The others may show before-and-after images, plus split views showing before and after in the same picture.

GET DRAMATIC BLACK-AND-WHITE
with Silver Efex Pro

Black-and-white photography is a real art. It is not simply a matter of changing a color picture to grayscale or a monochrome. It is about how different brightness values and colors in a photograph are changed to tones of gray.

Nik Software Color Efex Pro has some very good black-and-white effects that offer a lot of control over these tones of gray. But for the photographer who really wants to get the most out of black-and-white,

Nik Software Silver Efex Pro offers even more flexibility and control. The plug-in uses the same type of interface as other Nik Software programs. Silver Efex Pro adds controls that make it easier to look at how a color picture changes to black and white. Preset effects are shown as small sample images to make your options easier to choose. Just click what you want. In addition, there is a range of controls that enable you to make adjustments as needed.

Note: *To begin, click Filter, select Nik Software, and select Silver Efex Pro. Silver Efex Pro appears.*

● The adjustment that appears in the center pane is the default adjustment, Neutral.

❶ Examine the sample image thumbnails at the left side to see what looks good with your photo.

❷ Click the desired change and the center photo shows the adjustment.

❸ Revise this adjustment using the sliders at the upper right.

214

④ Click a color filter to change how colors translate to black and white.

⑤ Click Details.

⑥ Change the Hue slider to see how colors are affected.

DIFFICULTY LEVEL

⑦ Vary the Strength slider to adjust the effect.

⑧ Click the Add Control Point button.

⑨ Click something in the photograph that you want to adjust separately from the rest.

⑩ Change the Control Point sliders to affect that area.

⑪ Click OK.

Did You Know?

Structure in Silver Efex Pro is an adjustment that affects the finer gradations of tonalities. It is similar to Contrast, and definitely affects contrast, but it is a more refined control. Structure looks at and adjusts small midtone changes in tonalities for more or less drama in the details of a picture.

Did You Know?

Control points allow you to make very specific changes to your photograph without ever having to deal with layers or layer masks. In Silver Efex Pro, you can selectively control the tonality and structure of an object or area. This really helps you define parts of a photograph.

More Options!

Silver Efex Pro includes a Film Types section that enables you to simulate the looks of 18 black-and-white films. Many photographers still prefer the look of a specific black-and-white film they used when they shot using traditional cameras. This part of the plug-in allows you to try out some of these looks on your photograph.

Use FocalPoint for
EASY DEPTH-OF-FIELD EFFECTS

onOne Software (www.ononesoftware.com) is another company that makes photographer-friendly plug-ins for Photoshop and Photoshop Elements. FocalPoint is a plug-in that enables you to do some interesting effects with sharpness in your picture. A good technique for emphasizing your subject is to shoot with a very limited amount of sharpness in the photograph so that only the subject is sharp. This is called *selective focus*.

FocalPoint makes it a lot of fun to play around with selective focus and other depth-of-field effects. To duplicate some of these effects without the program would require an expensive tilt-and-shift lens. Plus, performing those effects at the time the picture is taken locks them into the image. With FocalPoint, you can change your depth-of-field effects quickly and easily in Photoshop Elements. The program uses a unique tool called the FocusBug, which literally allows you to click and drag your sharpness effects on the photograph.

① Click File.

② Select Automation Tools.

③ Select FocalPoint.

FocalPoint opens.

④ Click the FocusBug icon.

⑤ Click and drag the FocusBug to the subject area that you want to be sharp.

216

6 Click one of the four FocusBug legs with solid dots.

These control the size and rotation of the focus area.

7 Drag the sizing legs until the grid covers the area of your subject that you want to be sharp.

8 Click and drag the Amount leg to change the blur around your subject.

9 Adjust the Aperture controls to affect the appearance of your blur.

10 Click Apply.

 TIPS

Important!

You cannot add sharpness to a photograph. If you need something to be sharp in the picture, it must be sharp when you take the picture. FocalPoint needs sharpness to work with so that there is something to contrast against the blur. The plug-in can help a photograph with sharpness problems as long as the subject itself is sharp.

Did You Know?

You can readjust the legs of the FocusBug as much as you want as you go through the process of refining your blur. The two legs with open circles on them even enable you to adjust the blur amount and opacity while you are working on the image itself.

More Options!

FocalPoint offers some additional creative options for you. You can create a motion blur to make your subject look like it is moving quickly. You can also add a vignette to make the blurred areas lighter or darker. If the image has no blur, you can simply use the vignette to quickly and easily darken outside parts of the picture.

TRY PHOTOTUNE FOR
fast color and tonal adjustments

While it is true that Photoshop Elements has a good variety of controls to adjust the color and tones of your photo, sometimes it seems that they are too much of a good thing. Where do you start? Even if you know how to find them and use the controls from this book, you still have to think about what to do. How much of an adjustment do you make? How much of a change to color is appropriate to the subject?

PhotoTune from onOne Software is designed to focus on changes in your photo, not changes in sliders. The program gives you sample images with adjustments built into them that you choose, just like going to the eye doctor, where you choose which correction is better: a or b. The plug-in also comes in a Professional version designed to help pros with adjustments such as precise skin color and tone when doing portraits.

① Click Filter.

② Select onOne.

③ Select ColorTune.

● The ColorTune window appears.

④ Check to see how the image changes with a different dynamic range choice if needed.

⑤ Click the image you prefer to go to the next pair of images.

6 Keep clicking the best looking image of the two.

● A progress bar tracks your work.

7 Even if neither photo looks great, pick the best of the two.

8 Use the slider to increase or decrease the effect.

● When you have reached the last set of choices, you have arrived at the Fine-Tune panel.

● You will see a before-and-after of your image.

9 Click Apply to finish.

TIPS

Did You Know?

PhotoTune has a better saturation control than Photoshop Elements. The adjustment in Photoshop Elements is rather heavy handed and the overall adjustment affects colors equally whether they need it or not. PhotoTune's saturation control is available in the Basic tab of the Fine-Tune window and adjusts each color separately based on how saturated it is to start.

More Options!

SkinTune is a unique application of PhotoTune's processing algorithms that is specifically geared toward making skin tones look better. You click a skin tone, tell the program what kind of person this is, and then you get a set of adjustments designed to help you get the best skin tone and color from your subject.

Did You Know?

The Fine-Tune part of PhotoTune may seem counterproductive because it suddenly adds a lot of controls. You do not have to use any of them, but they are there if needed. The H&S tab is especially powerful for affecting color, specifically in highlight and shadow areas.

Use Enlarge It for
MAKING BIG PRINTS

High megapixels in a digital camera are not an indication of quality but of how big a picture can be printed. Higher megapixels also mean you can crop an image significantly and still get a good moderate-sized print. Not everyone can afford or even needs a high-megapixel digital camera. Also, low-priced point-and-shoot cameras with high megapixels do not have the image quality of lower-megapixel digital single lens reflex (dSLR) cameras.

Photoshop Elements has the capability to enlarge an image so that you can use a lower-megapixel camera or crop an image significantly and still get big prints. onOne Software's resizing plug-in Enlarge It is part of its Essentials 2 for Photoshop Elements. Enlarge It uses different algorithms than Photoshop Elements does to help resize images so they are bigger but still maintain sharp edges and small details. Small enlargements are fine in Photoshop Elements, but for big changes in size, it is better to use Enlarge It.

① Click File.

② Select Automation Tools.

③ Select Enlarge It.

Note: *Enlarge It will work with layered files.*

● Enlarge It opens.

● The key enlarging controls are set up similarly to the Resize controls in Photoshop Elements.

④ Click a height or width.

⑤ Type the desired size for that dimension and click the other dimension.

● The second dimension is automatically calculated as long as Constrain proportions is selected.

● A new image and file size appears in Pixel Dimensions.

⑥ Click Fit to fit the enlarged photo back on your screen.

⑦ Click the scrollbar to move the adjustment panel up and down.

Enlarging an image can cause softness you will need to correct by Sharpening.

⑧ Sharpen your photo by adjusting the Amount slider first.

⑨ Check your edges for halo effects — bright, unwanted edges — and reduce the Radius setting if needed.

⑩ Add Film Grain to smooth out extremely large enlargements.

⑪ Click Apply.

TIPS

Did You Know?

Essentials 2 for Photoshop Elements includes two other programs besides Enlarge It. Make It Better displays your photo twice side-by-side and makes adjustments to one so you can compare the original photo with the adjusted one. You simply click the one you like best, and then get two new versions to pick from. Cut It Out simplifies the process needed to cut a subject out from a background.

Did You Know?

When you enlarge an image, you typically need to sharpen it. This is why Enlarge It has a built-in sharpening tool. Enlarge It also includes adjustments to affect texture and the appearance of grain in the image, two areas that can be adversely affected by enlarging an image.

Check It Out!

onOne Software's Web site (www.ononesoftware.com) includes additional information about all of the company's plug-ins, including a very interesting program to add special-effect frames to your photos. Essentials 2 for Photoshop Elements simplifies three of onOne's Photoshop plug-ins to make them a better fit for Photoshop Elements users.

Chapter 10

Get Photos out of Photoshop Elements

One reason why people photograph is to share their experiences of the world with other people. Photoshop Elements offers a lot of great ways to do exactly that. Once you have done all of your work on your pictures in Photoshop Elements, you do not want to let them just sit there. Get them out so that people can view your pictures, share your experiences, and learn about your passions.

Today, you can share pictures with others in so many ways. There are online resources, including the Photoshop Elements Web site for users, Photoshop.com. You can print your pictures so you can share them with others in the traditional way of looking at a photograph. Displaying your photos on the wall is a great way to share your experiences with others.

You can create photo greeting cards based on your own pictures, add photographs to a CD or DVD, and make picture labels for your CDs and DVDs. Photos on a CD or DVD can include a slide show of your photographs that you can send to friends and relatives. Photoshop Elements makes it a lot of fun to be a photographer today!

Top 100

Gain more options
WITH PHOTOSHOP.COM

The Internet has become an increasingly important part of a photographer's world. Adobe created something entirely new for Photoshop Elements 7: a special members-only Web site for users of the program, and continues it with Elements 8. A Basic Membership is available for everyone who uses Photoshop Elements, whereas you can purchase the Plus Membership as part of the premium Adobe Photoshop Elements with the Photoshop.com package or purchase it later.

Basic Membership enables you to store up to 2GB of photos online, off of your computer. In addition, you gain access to the invitation-only Online Albums. With Online Albums, you upload images that your friends and family can open using a password. This enables you to easily work on images in Photoshop Elements and then get them quickly to a place where others can see them, too. Finally, any Photoshop.com membership enables you to view your uploaded photos from anywhere that you can access the Internet.

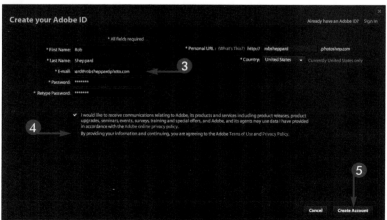

Note: Start by opening Photoshop Elements. You must have a computer connected to the Internet to continue.

① On the opening screen, click Create Adobe ID if you have never used Photoshop.com.

② If you have used Photoshop.com, type your Adobe ID and password in the lower-left corner, and then click Sign In.

The Adobe ID page opens.

③ Fill in the required information.

④ Select the Terms and Agreements statement (☐ changes to ☑).

⑤ Click Create Account.

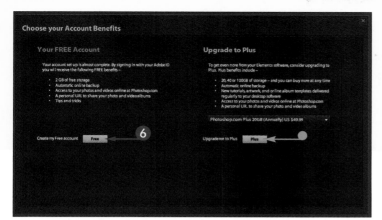

A verification notice appears asking you to check your e-mail and confirm your account.

Log in from that e-mail information.

The Membership Level page opens.

6 Click Free.

● You can click Plus, but there will be an additional charge.

The Account Created page opens, summarizing your account.

Your account is at the address you chose when you signed up.

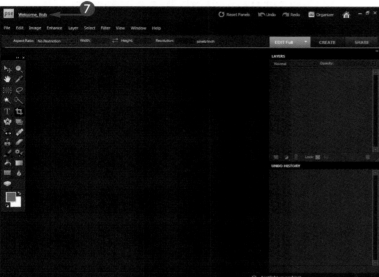

7 Check on your account at any time by clicking the Welcome link at the top of Photoshop Elements.

This tells you your Photoshop.com address and summarizes details of your account.

TIPS

Check It Out!

For more information on Photoshop.com for both the Plus and Basic Memberships, you can go to www.adobe.com and click the blue PSE Photoshop Elements icon. Or you can type **www.adobe.com/products/photoshopelwin/ membership** or **www.adobe.com/products/ photoshopelmac/membership** directly and click on Plus benefits. Both Web sites provide a complete comparison of Basic and Plus.

Did You Know?

Plus Membership offers you creative templates that are updated continually, seasonal artwork, tutorials, and interactive Online Album templates. These can be fun ways to work with Photoshop Elements, though not every photographer is going to find them useful.

Did You Know?

When comparing Plus and Basic storage, you cannot simply use Adobe's numbers. There is no such thing as a standard JPEG file, so all storage numbers must be qualified. Basic's 2GB is a very low number and can be used only for a limited number of photos. Plus's 20GB obviously offers you ten times the storage.

PROTECT YOUR PHOTOS
with online backup

Backing up your photos is very important. Although neither the 2GB available for the Basic Membership of Photoshop.com nor the 20GB for Plus can replace an accessory hard drive, this online backup can serve a very useful purpose. You can keep special archived images here separate from your home files. Hopefully, you never experience fire, floods, hurricanes, tornadoes, or any other disaster, but should any disaster happen, you will have the images backed up online.

You can certainly back up any of your photos at any time. This works best if you are only shooting JPEG images. If you shoot RAW, your online backup fills in a hurry. You will get the most from the Photoshop.com online backup by creating a special album for backup files and then saving finished images there as JPEGs. This is a fine use of JPEG: as an archival format to keep files small for storage.

Note: To begin, open your Web browser.

① Go to www.photoshop.com.

② Sign in with your e-mail address and password

③ Click Sign In to log in to your account.

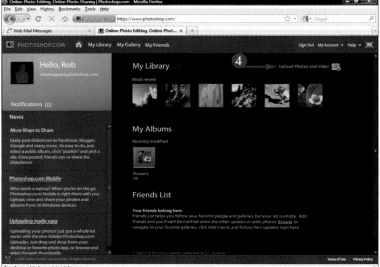

Your storage site appears.

④ Click Upload Photos and Video.

94

The Select files window opens.

5 Click the Look in drop-down menu to navigate to the picture folder you want to back up.

6 Select the photos you want.

7 Click Open.

DIFFICULTY LEVEL

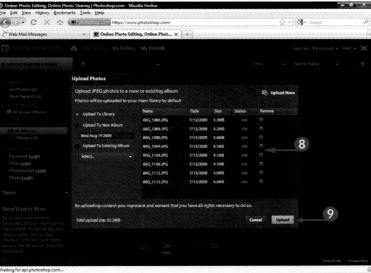

The Upload Photos window appears.

8 Check to be sure your photos are correct for uploading.

9 Click Upload.

Your photos are uploaded for storage on Photoshop.com.

 TIPS

Caution!

Never rely only on one form of backup, especially only one online. Even if you could get enough storage space online, you would always have to have online access to use that storage. Although online access is fairly reliable, it is never as reliably accessible as a hard drive plugged directly into your computer.

Try This!

JPEG files are excellent for archival backup because they let you reduce the size of your photos. Keep your photo compression low; that is, Quality set to 8 or higher in the JPEG Save options box. These should be files you have finished working on. Avoid reprocessing already-processed JPEG files. If you want to save an unprocessed file, you can use JPEG, and then save it as a TIFF (Tagged Image File Format) or PSD (Photoshop Document) file if the JPEG is opened for processing and you need to resave the file.

More Options!

If you are connected to the Internet, Photoshop Elements continues to give you messages about things available on Photoshop.com and other offers. To change this, go to the Edit menu and choose Preferences and then Adobe Partner Services. You can select or deselect the options Adobe sends you from a whole series under Check for Services.

ACCESS YOUR PHOTOS
anywhere Internet service is available

You can access online storage anywhere that you have Internet access. If you travel a lot, this is a great way to access your photos from a distance. Even if you do not have a laptop with you, you can access your photos using someone else's computer or even the guest computer at a hotel.

In addition, very small, compact laptops, the so-called "Web computers," are becoming popular with travelers. Designed for the ubiquitous Internet access

that has become a part of the world today, Web computers have limited storage space built into the units. Because storage is restricted, you cannot store a lot of photos on them. Online photo storage makes great use of these computers.

Finally, many business travelers have no need to take their photos with them, but it is nice to access special images, such as those of family, friends, and events while on the road.

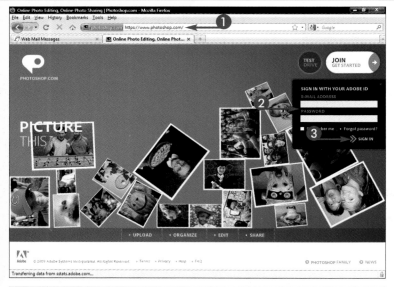

1 Go to www.photoshop.com.

The login box appears.

2 Sign in with your e-mail address and password.

3 Click Sign In.

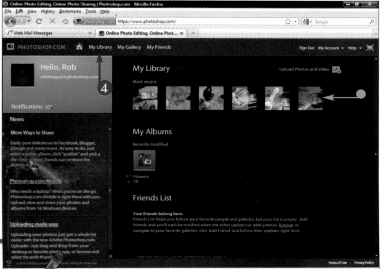

Your Photoshop.com account appears.

● Your most recent photos show up as thumbnails.

How many photos show up depends on how many you have uploaded.

4 Click My Library.

Your photos are now accessible for work.

5 Click the sizing boxes to change the size of the thumbnails.

6 Hover your cursor over a photo to access Photo Options for a photo.

7 Click the down arrow for Photo Options to get a contextual menu of options.

8 Double-click a photo to work on it remotely.

The photo then appears as a single image.

9 Click any toolbar icon to work with your photo.

The toolbar is intuitive and lets you edit your photo, e-mail it, decorate it, print it, and so on.

10 Click the Home icon to return to your complete library of photos at Photoshop.com.

 TIPS

Did You Know?

If you find you are running out of room for your photos, you can always rent additional space. Click My Account and then Account Settings at the upper right of your Photoshop.com page. This opens an account summary. Click the Buy More button at the right of your storage slider.

Try This!

Photoshop.com is set up for sharing and makes it easy for you to do this. You can create a Friends List. This gives you immediate notification if anyone on this list updates galleries or adds images to her Photoshop.com account. You can set up your Friends List after browsing other public galleries, and you can interact with people who have photography you like.

Did You Know?

My Library, My Gallery, and My Friends are three buttons that give quick access to certain parts of Photoshop.com. My Library shows you all your images and lets you work on them, including moving or deleting them. My Gallery displays your photos in the gallery theme you choose; this is the gallery others see. My Friends lets you browse other photographers' public galleries.

Create online
PHOTO ALBUMS

Just like you did in the Organizer, you can create albums or special collections of your photos in your Photoshop.com library. When you upload images directly to Photoshop.com, they enter the library, which only gives you very basic organization. Albums not only let you group and find specific photos faster, but they also enable you to help friends and relatives find them. Albums have no effect on your photos on Photoshop.com other than to group them. Photos can go in more than one album, too, which gives you

great options for organizing them online. You can group photos by type, event, people, and so on.

Albums are a key part of your Photoshop.com image storage. You need albums in order to use many of the sharing features, such as galleries. You can have an album open to everyone, open only to friends, or private.

Note: To begin, open your Photoshop.com account and click My Photos on the opening page.

① Click All Photos in your library to make them visible.

② Choose from a size icon so the pictures are small and you can see many at once.

③ Click Show to access a menu that controls what is displayed with your photos.

④ Press Ctrl/Cmd while you click several photos to make a selection of them.

⑤ Click and drag them onto the green plus (+) sign, which is the new folder icon.

● A new plus sign appears when you are directly over the folder.

⑥ Release the images by releasing the mouse button.

A New Album window appears.

7 Type a name for the album

8 Select an option for who is allowed to see this album online.

9 Click Create.

DIFFICULTY LEVEL

● Your album is created and now shows up in your library.

TIPS

Did You Know?

You can create an instant slide show of your photos when they are in an album. Once you open an album, you will find a Slideshow icon in the toolbar at the bottom of the screen; click that icon to create a slide show from that album. This creates a fun, 3D, rotating slide show with an option panel on the right.

Try This!

You can also set up an album without selecting photos. While in the library, click the Create Album icon in the toolbar at the bottom of your screen, and then select New Album. This enables you to set up and name an album. You can then go through your library and drag photos onto the name of your new album to add photos to the album.

More Options!

You can upload an album directly when you create an album in the Organizer. Be sure that Backup/Synchronize is selected when the Album Details panel is open and you are setting up a new album. When you click Share, you get a series of options to choose as you prep your album for upload.

SHARE YOUR PHOTOS
online

One of the joys of photography is sharing photography with others. On a most basic level, people like to see what others are doing, whether it is grandparents viewing photos of grandkids playing soccer or a businessperson in one geographic location showing how a retail store looks to an associate elsewhere. Plus, when big events occur, such as weddings, family reunions, and births, people love to see the visual record.

Everyone sees the world differently, and photography is a way of expressing those unique visions. Yet, if you keep those photos only on your computer, no one else can benefit from your point of view. Photoshop.com gives you the chance to share photos with not only friends and neighbors, but also people who share your love of photography. You have total control, too, of how people access your photos so you never have to worry about the wrong people seeing specific photos.

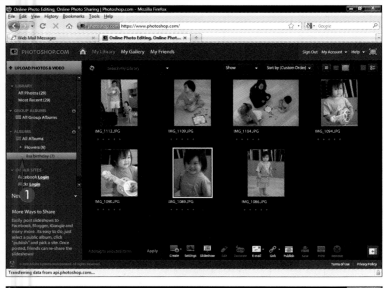

Note: To begin, open your Photoshop.com account and click Library on the opening page.

❶ Click the small dot to the left of the album name.

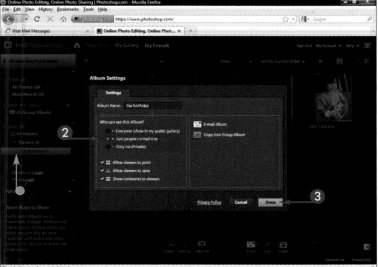

The Album Settings window appears.

❷ Choose how you want to share your album.

❸ Click Done.

● The dot in front of your album changes color based on your sharing choice.

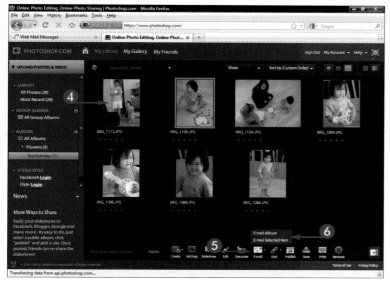

④ Click a photo.

⑤ Click the E-mail icon in the bottom toolbar.

⑥ Choose either E-mail Album or E-mail Selected Item to e-mail friends or relatives a link to your photo or album.

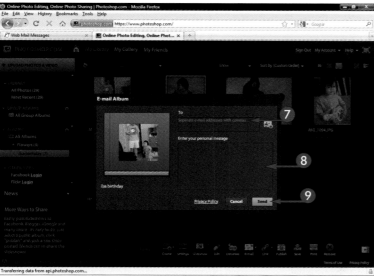

The E-mail dialog box appears.

⑦ Type the e-mail addresses of the people to whom you want to send a link to your photos.

⑧ Type a message to let recipients know about your album and that it is not spam.

⑨ Click Send.

TIPS

More Options!

You can personalize your gallery space with a photo of you as well as personal information. When you are in My Gallery, open your overall gallery section. You will find a place to add your personal photo, as well as information that appears when an album is permitted for public view, such as a personal tagline and gallery description.

Caution!

You might be tempted to back up within Photoshop.com by using the Back button on your Internet browser. Do not do it! That takes you off of Photoshop.com and you have to log in again. To move within Photoshop.com, only click links on your pages. You can navigate to library photos, galleries, albums, and more right there.

More Options!

Photoshop.com gives you several sharing options for albums. "Everyone" puts your photos into a public gallery, and anyone who uses Photoshop.com can browse the site and find your album. "Just people I e-mail it to or invite to it" allows anyone you permit to view your album, but no public viewing is allowed. "Only me" means that only you can access your album.

PRINT
your photos

With all the emphasis these days on seeing pictures on the Internet, on iPods, by e-mail, and other electronic media, one might think that the print is no longer important. That is definitely not the case. Inkjet printers are extremely popular, and paper and ink continue to be sold in large quantities.

And there is something more. The print has a real psychological aura to it. People love looking at prints, holding prints, sharing prints, putting them into frames and up on the wall, and so on. Prints are important. And photographers are making them bigger and bigger.

This book cannot make you a master printer, but the next four pages give you some ideas on how you can make better prints with your own inkjet printer. Photo-quality inkjet printers are available today at very reasonable prices all the way up to expensive pro-level printers.

Note: *Start by sizing and sharpening the photo as discussed in Chapter 7.*

● The width and height are important at a printable image resolution of 200–360 ppi.

① Click File and select Print.

The Print dialog box opens.

② Click the orientation icons to change vertical or horizontal use of the image.

③ Click the Select Printer drop-down menu if you have more than one printer and select the printer to use from the menu.

④ Click Change Settings in Printer Settings.

The Change Settings dialog box appears.

⑤ Choose the correct paper type based on what you are using.

⑥ Choose the paper size that you are using.

⑦ Click OK.

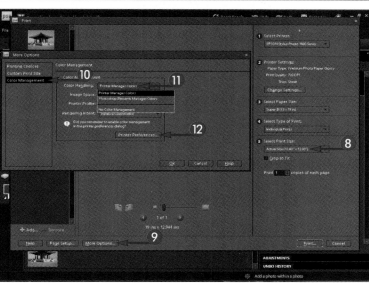

⑧ Click the Select Print Size to set a size for the image on the paper.

⑨ Click More Options.

⑩ Click Color Management.

⑪ Click the Color Handling drop-down menu to choose Printer Manages Colors or Photoshop Elements Manages Colors.

Canon and Hewlett-Packard, as well as lower-priced Epson printers, often do well with Printer Manages Colors.

Higher-end Epson printers usually do best with Photoshop Elements Manages Colors.

⑫ If you chose Printer Manages Colors in step 11, click Printer Preferences now.

TIPS

Important!
Calibrating your monitor is important. Monitor calibration is done using a special sensor that fits on your monitor screen and reads colors and tones from calibration software. A calibrated monitor gives you a predictable and consistent environment for working on images that will become prints.

Did You Know?
When the printer manages color, it takes the color information from Photoshop Elements and refines it based on the paper used and the color settings of the printer driver. When Photoshop Elements manages color, a very specific interpretation of color is sent to the printer based on paper profiles.

Did You Know?
Printer profiles are specific translations of color and tonality for printing based on testing specific papers with specific printers. They are also called *paper profiles*. A special image of colors is printed on paper, and then the colors are read and interpreted by colorimeters in order to define a profile.

PRINT
your photos

You often hear photographers say that their goal is to make a print that matches the monitor. Although it is important to have a calibrated monitor that gives predictable results when printing, your goal should be to make a good *print*. No one will care if it matches the monitor or not. A viewer cares only about the print in front of him.

This is a different mindset than many digital photographers work with. It means that you have to take your print away from the monitor and really look at it as a print. Do you like the image that you see? Does it have the appropriate brightness and balance of tonalities for the size of the print? Are there color casts that show up too strongly in a print but looked okay on the monitor? What you are looking for is a print that you can be proud to put up on the wall.

⑬ If you chose Photoshop Elements Manages Colors in step 11, click the Printer Profile drop-down menu.

A profile menu appears.

⑭ Select the profile that fits your printer and paper.

⑮ Click Printer Preferences, which is visible when the Printer Profile menu closes.

The printer driver appears.

Important: *The driver interface varies depending on the printer model and your operating system, but you must set the same things.*

The Properties dialog box sets most of the settings for you, but you want to confirm them and will need to work with an additional setting here.

⑯ Select the correct printing quality option.

⑰ Confirm the paper type.

⑱ Confirm the paper size.

⑲ Click Advanced.

Important! *The following settings appear in different places for various printer models and Macs or PCs, so you may have to look for them.*

20 If you chose Printer Manages Colors in step 11, leave Color Controls selected in the Color Management section.

21 If you chose Photoshop Elements Manages Colors in step 11, select ICM and Off (No Color Adjustment) (or No Color Management in some printer drivers) in the Color Management section.

22 Click OK.

23 Click OK to close the More Options dialog box.

24 Choose a number of prints to make.

25 Click Crop to Fit if you want the photo itself to fit a specific paper size.

26 Click Print.

TIPS

Try This!

Photographers using traditional darkrooms almost always consider their first print a work print. They examine this print carefully to decide what else is needed to make the print better. Many photographers consider a work print a good idea for digital printing as well.

Did You Know?

Although you can use Scale Print Size to make a picture fit a certain size of paper, use this sparingly. It works if you are making only a small change in size. For optimum quality, you need to size the picture with the specific resizing algorithms used inside Photoshop Elements itself.

Did You Know?

Printer resolution and image resolution are two different things. *Printer resolution* is set by the printer driver and affects how ink droplets are put on the paper. *Image resolution* is set by Photoshop Elements and is based on the pixels in the photograph. There is little direct relationship between the two.

PRINT A GROUP
of photos

There are times when you want to print more than one photograph at once. Sometimes you simply want a number of pictures to represent a recent trip. Or you may want to print several photos on a single sheet of printing paper to make your printing more efficient.

This is very easy to do within the Organizer. In the Organizer, you see all your pictures from an album or a particular time and then choose the pictures that you want to print using the rating stars. It can be hard to select a variety of pictures throughout a large group of images. But you can click the individual pictures that you want to use and then give each one a rating, such as three stars. You then simply sort your images so those three-star pictures appear in the window. You can quickly process each one for optimum image quality and then select them all for printing.

① Mark the photos to print by giving them a star rating.

② Sort the rated pictures by clicking the star sorting bar.

Note: See task #4 for more about sorting.

③ Click File.

④ Select Print.

⑤ Click Yes in the confirmation dialog box that appears.

The Prints dialog box appears.

All the choices you made for a single print are also made here.

⑥ Click the Change Settings drop-down menu and choose your paper.

⑦ Click the Select Paper Size drop-down menu and choose your paper size.

⑧ Click the orientation icons to orient your picture and paper to vertical or horizontal.

⑨ Click the Select Print Size drop-down menu and choose the size to print based on your image size.

⑩ Click the Select Type of Print drop-down menu and choose Picture Package.

⑪ Click the Select a Layout drop-down menu and choose the layout that you want for your pictures.

● As soon as you select an option from Select a Layout, it appears in the center display.

To have the printer manage colors, simply click Print.

⑫ Click More Options to print with Photoshop Elements managing colors.

The More Options dialog box appears.

⑬ Click Color Management if more than one choice shows.

⑭ Click the Print Space drop-down menu and choose the paper profile for your paper and printer.

● Same as Source restores the default of having the printer manage colors.

TIPS

Keyboard Trick!
Ctrl/Cmd+P is the standard keyboard command for print. It enables you to print a picture whether you are in Editor or Organizer. In Editor, it takes you directly to the single-picture Print dialog box. A multiple-print button is also there. In Organizer, pressing Ctrl/Cmd+P takes you directly to the multiple-print Print Photos dialog box.

Important!
It is very tempting to put in a specific-size print for Select Print Size and Options. If your image has not been sized close to a size that you are choosing, you will not get optimum quality. This is especially true if you are making larger prints. For small casual prints, having Print Photos size your pictures is fine.

Did You Know?
When you print in Photoshop Elements, you have some additional options. For example, a popular choice is creating an iron-on transfer. To do a transfer, you need special paper and a flipped image. Rather than making you flip the original shot, a printing choice is available, called Flip Image in Iron-on Transfer, that does it for the print only.

Make a photo
GREETING CARD

As a digital photographer, you take a lot of pictures. After all, it costs nothing to take pictures digitally once you own the camera and memory card. But what do you do with all those pictures? One way of using your pictures is to create your own greeting cards based on your photographs.

This gives a personal touch to a greeting card. You can make greeting cards for events such as birthdays or seasons such as Christmas. You can create cards that have unique photographs for each recipient, or you can create cards with a standard image that you really like a lot. Customizing these cards is also easy: You can add text appropriate to the event or something special for the recipient of the card. You can even set up a card and save it so that you can reuse it in the future with slight changes.

① Click the Create tab.

② Click the Projects tab and select Greeting Card.

An intermediate panel opens.

③ Select Print with Local printer to print your own greeting card.

④ Select one of the other two options to use the Internet to have a lab print your card.

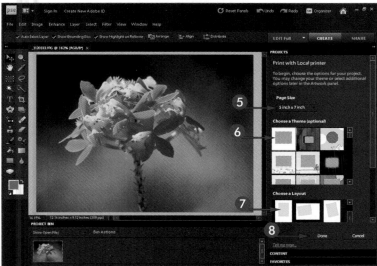

The Greeting Card panel appears.

⑤ Choose a page size for your card.

⑥ Choose a theme by clicking the thumbnail.

This affects how your image appears and what is around it.

⑦ Choose a layout by clicking a thumbnail.

This affects the way your picture is arranged on the page.

⑧ Click Done.

The photo is now displayed as a card based on your theme and layout choices, but it probably comes in cropped because it is too large.

#100

⑨ Right-click the photo and select Position Photo in Frame.

⑩ Click and drag the slider and the small boxes on the bounding box to change the size of the photo in the frame area.

⑪ Click the green check mark when you are done.

⑫ Click the Move tool, and then click and drag the framed photo to position it on the card.

⑬ Click the drop-down menu on the right in the Content tab and select Text.

⑭ Click and drag a text style to the card.

⑮ Double-click the text to access the text options bar.

⑯ Change any text attribute in the options bar.

⑰ Click the Move tool to reposition and size the text.

⑱ Save your work as a PSD file.

TIPS

Try This!
If you save your greeting card as a PSD file with layers, you can always go back and revise your text. A text layer can be changed at any time. Simply go to the Edit Full tab, and then double-click the T icon in the layer and your text is selected. This enables you to use the standard greeting, for example, and then personalize a name.

Important!
Process your photo first before you create a greeting card. You want your pictures to look their best when printed out as greeting cards. In order to do this, do your processing in the Edit tab the way you would work on any photograph.

More Options!
Text works the way it does in a text program like Word. The options bar has all the text-editing standard features, including ones for choosing a font, the size of the font, the alignment of text, and a color. In addition, you can select a style, curve the text, and run the text vertically.

Create
PHOTO COLLAGES

Photo collages are a way of putting together multiple pictures on a page. This can be an interesting way of showing off an event on, for example, a single page. Similarly, you can put single shots of all the players from a kids' soccer team on a single page. This can make a great print that can be shared with the entire team. Photoshop Elements makes this easy to do.

In addition, scrapbooking has become a popular way of working with multiple photographs on a

page — which is exactly what a photo collage is. You can even buy photo paper sized to scrapbook proportions for printing.

Photoshop Elements enables you to have some fun with multiple pictures on a page, whether you are putting together a scrapbook or just creating a fun collage. This task introduces this topic; you will find a lot of things to do with collages once you start working with them.

Create a Collage

1️⃣ Open several photos from the Organizer in the Editor.

2️⃣ Click Create.

3️⃣ Click the Projects tab.

4️⃣ Click Photo Collage.

The Photo Collage panel appears.

5️⃣ Choose a page size for your collage.

6️⃣ Choose a theme by clicking a thumbnail.

7️⃣ Choose a layout by clicking a thumbnail.

8️⃣ Click Done.

The photos are now displayed in a collage based on your theme and layout choices, but are cropped because they are too large.

DIFFICULTY LEVEL

⑨ Right-click a photo and select Position Photo in Frame.

⑩ Click and drag the slider and the small boxes on the bounding box to change the size of the photo in the frame area.

⑪ Click the green check mark when you are done.

⑫ Fix all the photos.

⑬ Click the Move tool in the small toolbox.

⑭ Click and drag photos to new positions.

⑮ Click and drag the small boxes on the bounding box of a photo to change its size.

⑯ Click the green check mark when you are done.

TIPS

More Options!

The Move tool has a number of important options. When you check Auto Select Layer, the correct layer (which is a photo in the collage) is automatically selected when you click an object in that layer. When you select Show Highlight on Rollover, any object within a layer shows up with a blue box around it to help you find the right layer.

Did You Know?

Photo Collage, like the Greeting Card feature, creates something called a *layer style* to give the edges of the photograph a unique look. Layer styles influence the way an image is displayed, but do not change the actual photograph. This allows you to change an image in a layer and still keep the layer style.

More Options!

Experiment with the Themes and Layout options. When you click options, a small image appears, showing you what the theme or layout looks like, but you really cannot tell how they will work with your pictures until you try them. So try them! See what they look like. If you do not like the effect, close the picture and start over again. This takes little time to do, but is worth the effort.

Create
PHOTO COLLAGES

A collage has long been a way of working with photographs. But in the past, you had to cut up pictures and then paste them onto a page. That definitely created problems if you wanted to make any changes!

By working your collage in Photoshop Elements, you can do some quite elegant work. You can move your pictures around, resize them, or add or take away photos, and nothing is hurt or damaged in any way. This is very important because in order to get a good

collage, you need to think a bit about how photos go together. Which photos look good next to each other? Which photos fight with each other and need some separation?

Work your collage with variety with respect to the sizes of images. A big photo or two makes a nice contrast to smaller ones. In addition, resist the impulse to include everything in one page. That can look cluttered and makes it hard for a viewer to focus on the images.

17 Click the Edit Full tab.

The Edit Full panel appears.

● Your photographs are now in layers.

18 Click the Move tool in the toolbox.

19 Click and drag a layer to move it up or down in the layer stack.

This also changes how a photograph overlaps the others.

Add a Photo by Duplicating a Layer

20 Click a layer.

21 Drag it to the New Layer icon at the bottom left of the Layers palette.

- The layer is duplicated.

㉒ Click and drag the photo to a new position on the collage.

㉓ Click the photo in the Project Bin that you want to add to the collage.

㉔ Drag it on top of the duplicate photo you want to replace.

- A plus (+) sign appears when the cursor is in the proper position over the photo.

  The photo now replaces the duplicated image.

- The sizing bar appears.

㉕ Move the sizing slider to change the size of your image within the picture frame.

㉖ Click the green check mark.

  You can move the photos around using the Move tool or by moving the layers up or down in the Layers palette.

TIPS

More Options!
You have seen how the Move tool can help you resize your photographs in the collage. Be sure Show Bounding Box is selected so that when you click the photograph, a bounding box with little boxes at the corners appears. Click and drag any of those little boxes to enlarge or shrink the photograph. Click outside the bounding box and drag to rotate the picture.

Did You Know?
It can take a bit of work to get a collage to look right. As photographs overlap each other, sometimes they cover up the wrong parts of the picture. Try moving pictures up and down in the layer stack to see how they overlap, and what is better or worse. Then use the Move tool to move the pictures around in the collage until they look their best.

Did You Know?
An interesting group of thumbnails that represents the collage appears in the Project Bin. You see the entire process of the collage in miniature. You can double-click any of these thumbnails to see an earlier stage of the collage.

ADD FRAME EFFECTS
to your pictures

You can apply some very interesting effects to the edges of your picture in Photoshop Elements. You can create realistic-looking frames, colorful borders and mattes, funky edges, and a whole lot more. All of these effects are applied to your picture as layers, too, which means that they are nondestructive. You cannot hurt your original picture, no matter how unusual an edge effect might be. So experiment freely.

Watch how edges interact with your photograph. You do not want a frame effect to be more dramatic than your picture. One problem a lot of photographers run into is that they pick a color for a matte that competes with the colors in the photograph. Another problem is that an edge color can be too similar to the colors in your photograph and pull visual energy from the image. Choose edges that complement the photograph.

1. Click the Create tab.
2. Click the Content tab.
3. Select By Type under Content.
4. Select Frames to the right of By Type.

   The Frames panel appears.

5. Position your cursor over a frame to get a description of it.
6. Double-click a frame thumbnail to try it out.

   The frame appears around your subject.

● This image has been created as a layer, so blank areas show up as a checkerboard pattern.

246

7 Position your cursor over additional frames and edges to see what they are.

8 Double-click the frame thumbnail to replace your last frame.

● Alternately, right-click a frame thumbnail and then click Apply to Document.

9 Click Edit Full when you have an effect that you like.

● The Edit Full panel appears with the photo now in a single layer.

10 Click the background color.

Choose white in the Color Picker (Background Color) dialog box.

11 Click Layer

12 Select Flatten Image.

The background color now fills the checkerboard area as the image is flattened.

TIPS

Important!
In order to use frames on your picture, you must have a flattened photograph or at least a pixel layer. Frames give you very odd effects if you work on a standard layered file. Frames are applied to whatever layer is active, but you may not necessarily like the effect.

More Options!
Because frames are applied to a layer using layer styles, you can repeatedly use a frame with other photos. Save the photo with the layer. Open a new photo. Drag that photo from the Project Bin onto the framed photo. A large plus (+) sign shows you that you are doing this right. The new photo replaces the old one in the frame.

Check It Out!
If you like interesting frame and edge effects, check out PhotoFrame from onOne Software (www.ononesoftware.com). This plug-in includes hundreds of frames that were developed by professional photographers but are now available for anyone to use. This plug-in works in Photoshop Elements.

Chapter 10: Get Photos out of Photoshop Elements

Make a
SLIDE SHOW

What do you do with all of the photographs that you have taken? You may print a few, or maybe put some on your iPod or iPhone. Because taking pictures digitally costs nothing, you may take a lot of pictures that never get used. Slide shows let you use more pictures as you share your experiences with others. Photoshop Elements helps you make a slide show that can be used on a computer or projected with one of the latest digital projectors.

Slide shows have a long tradition with photographers. They are perfect for sharing an event, such as a party or a trip, such as that vacation to the Grand Canyon. A key to a good slide show is to keep it simple. Avoid trying to put every single picture into the slide show. Edit your pictures down to the ones that really matter and then make sure to process them correctly.

Select Photos in the Organizer

1 Select an album.

2 Select images by giving them a star rating, such as three stars.

3 Sort your images to just the rated ones by clicking the star number on the rating icon.

Create a Slide Show

1 Click the Create tab.

2 Click Slide Show.

Slide Show Preferences appears.

3 Choose a duration for how long each slide appears.

4 Choose a transition between slides.

5 Choose a duration for transitions between slides.

103

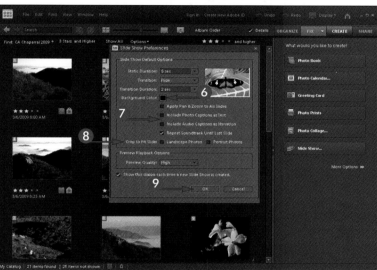

6 Click the Background Color to change the background behind the slide.

7 Deselect the captions options unless you have captions in the metadata that must be included.

8 Leave the Crop to Fit Slide options unchecked.

9 Click OK.

The Slide Show Editor appears.

TIPS

Try It!
A good way to work with slide shows is to create a special album in the Organizer specifically for them. This helps you keep your images organized and separated from other similar photographs. Rate your pictures, sort them by rating, select them, and put them into the album.

Did You Know?
Timing in a slide show is affected by the length of time a slide is up, the type of transition, and the length of the transition. A good place to start is with a slide duration of 4–6 seconds, which you can type into the box, and a fade transition of 1 second. You can make these shorter for a livelier show with fast music, or longer for a mellow show with slower music.

More Options!
Pan and zoom is a way of creating some movement with your pictures. Photoshop Elements zooms into certain parts of your picture, pans along an image, zooms out, and so on to create movement. Give it a try to see if you like it. You can also set this manually for individual slides in the Slide Show Editor.

Make a
SLIDE SHOW

A slide show should never be simply a group of random photos thrown together. Slide shows look their best with a definite beginning, middle, and end. Even if all of the pictures are of one subject, such as the natural area of chaparral shown here, you still need a picture to use for the first image and the last image, and some sort of logical progression between the images.

You can click and drag any of the images in the Slide Show Editor to new positions. You can use the set of playback buttons underneath the large window in the Slide Show Editor to preview your slide show without having to output it. This can help you see how transitions are working, if the slides are on too long or too briefly, and if you need to rearrange pictures. Take the time to play back your images as you work on your slide show to make sure that the images go together well.

⑩ Click the Text icon in Extras.

⑪ Drag a font onto the image.

● The Edit Text dialog box appears.

⑫ Type your text.

⑬ Click OK.

⑭ Click and drag your text into position.

⑮ Change the text with the options by clicking Edit Text under Properties.

⑯ Click the audio track that says Click Here to Add Audio to Your Slide Show.

● The Choose your audio files window appears.

⑰ Choose the audio file that you want to use as music for your slide show.

⑱ Click Open.

● The music appears in the audio track.

⑲ Click Save Project.

⑳ Name your slide show.

㉑ Click Save.

This saves your project so it can be reedited in the future.

㉒ Click Output to use your slide show.

㉓ Click Save As a File to have the finished slide show saved in its own file.

The slide show saved as Save As a File is a finished show and cannot be reedited.

㉔ Choose Movie File to play the slide show as a movie with all slide show features (○ changes to ●).

㉕ Choose a size for your slide show.

㉖ Click OK.

TIPS

More Options!

The Slide Show Editor includes a section in Extras that enables you to add clip art to your slide show. These are mostly little cartoon figures that some photographers like and some do not. But if you want to create a fun slide show about kids, for example, you may find the perfect addition here.

Try It!

You can create a DVD directly from the Slide Show Editor that plays back your slide show on someone else's computer or in a DVD player. Be aware, however, that DVDs do not always play on everyone's DVD player, especially if the DVD player is older.

Check It Out!

Although you can use any music you want for a personal slide show, you cannot simply use any music for public slide shows. You can use a lot of music on the Internet if you are sure that it is copyright free. Or check out SmartSound (www.smartsound. com), which offers music that can be created to specific lengths and used as needed.

Put your photos
ON A DVD OR CD

Recording files to a DVD or CD is an excellent way of getting a lot of images from your computer or transporting very large photo files from your computer to some other location. For example, it can take a long time to upload a large group of photos to the Internet, yet you can put those same photos on a disc quickly. Using the Internet to upload photos is a big problem if you want to get your photos to a lab

for printing big prints. Such photos usually mean very large file sizes.

A DVD can handle more than 4GB of data, which is a lot of photos, or a significant number of large image files. A CD is much smaller at approximately 700MB. Either disc is a convenient way to distribute your photo files, either to relatives or to a photo lab for printing.

❶ Select a group of photos in the Organizer that you want to burn to a disc.

● You might use a special album for this.

❷ Click the Share tab.

The Share panel appears.

❸ Click the Burn data CD/DVD button.

The Burn data CD/DVD dialog box appears.

④ Click the disc drive.

You must click your drive even if you have only one.

⑤ Type a short name for your disc.

⑥ Click OK.

A status window appears, depending on the disc-burning software in your computer.

A verification dialog box appears when the disc is complete.

⑦ Click Verify.

104

DIFFICULTY LEVEL

TIPS

Important!

If you plan on storing your photos on a disc for any length of time, do not use RW, or rewritable discs. Use only R (or recordable) discs. RW discs are made to change — that is what makes them rewritable. You do not want a disc of your photos to change unless you are using the disc only to transfer photos to another computer immediately. RW discs are not recommended at all for long-term storage.

Did You Know?

You can use recordable discs for archival storage of images. You are limited as to the number of photos that fit on a disc, so JPEG is a good format for your images. Use archival R discs, such as those from Delkin or Verbatim. Ordinary, cheap office-supply discs are not recommended for archival storage.

Caution!

Never put standard, rectangular labels on CD or DVD discs. Discs spin at high speeds in a drive. A label must be attached to the disc so that the disc remains balanced. An unbalanced disc can damage your drive. Either write information on the disk with a marker (and archival markers help) or carefully apply a circular disc printed label. These are the best ways to keep a CD or DVD balanced in the drive.

Index

Index

Index

Index

Index